INVENTORS

PROFILES IN CANADIAN GENIUS

THOMAS CARPENTER

CAMDEN HOUSE

Canadian Cataloguing in Publication Data

Carpenter, Thomas, 1959-
    Inventors: profiles in Canadian genius

ISBN 0-920656-95-1 (bound) ISBN 0-920656-93-5 (pbk.)

1. Inventors – Canada – Biography – Juvenile literature. 2. Inventions – Canada – History – Juvenile literature. I. Title.

T39.C37 1990   j609.22   C90-093908-7

Cover illustration by
Rocco Baviera

Trade distribution by
Firefly Books
250 Sparks Avenue
Willowdale, Ontario
Canada M2H 2S4

Printed and bound in Canada by
D.W. Friesen & Sons Ltd.
Altona, Manitoba, for
Camden House Publishing
(a division of Telemedia Publishing Inc.)
7 Queen Victoria Road
Camden East, Ontario K0K 1J0

Designed by
Linda J. Menyes

Colour separations by
Hadwen Graphics
Ottawa, Ontario

ACKNOWLEDGEMENTS

This book was written with the generous support of the Secretary of State whose Canadian Studies Directorate provided financial assistance and did so in a straightforward and encouraging manner.

I want to thank George Vosper, who gave liberally of his time and patiently explained the more complex details of Reginald Fessenden's accomplishments. I also wish to express my appreciation to researcher Christopher Baird and to Laurel Aziz for her assistance.

And finally, thank you to Camden House publisher Frank B. Edwards, who originally fostered the idea for this book and made its writing possible, and to staff members: editor Tracy C. Read; art director Linda Menyes; assistant editor Charlotte DuChene; copy editor Catherine DeLury; typesetter Patricia Denard-Hinch; editorial assistant Jane Good; publishing coordinator Mirielle Keeling; production manager Susan Dickinson; and associates Margo Stahl, Lois Casselman, Mary Patton, Christine Kulyk, Ellen Brooks Mortfield, Mary-Anne O'Connor, Peggy Denard and Johanna Troyer.

CONTENTS

INTRODUCTION

Inventors are enchanted by ideas, beguiled into following a trail of investigation to its very end. Though often a curse, their tenacious curiosity is nonetheless their greatest attribute, and if the inventors described in this book share only a single, essential characteristic, it is this: they possessed a grand capacity for fascination and allowed it to lead them to discovery.

The popular image of the inventor is of a messy, addlebrained dabbler who, through a single revelatory insight, miraculously finds himself or herself in a new realm of human knowledge. Yet nothing could be further from the truth; invention is not an event but a process. The inventions of the people whose lives are recorded here emerged from the work and determination of real people. Some of them saw the steady increase of their wealth and comfort. Others followed a harder road, marred by confusion and setbacks. In every case, however, their achievements were the consequence of dedicated, often tedious work, rather than magical inspiration.

The harder road travelled by Georges-Édouard Desbarats, who introduced the printed photograph to the world of journalism, cost him two fortunes, his own and his father's. Material success came easily to Thomas Willson, the inventor of acetylene, but Willson remained a man driven by his own insatiable curiosity about new technologies. Abraham Gesner died unrecognized for the contributions he made to the petrochemical industry, and while he lived, his family often faced adversity and displacement as a consequence of his restless inquiries. Helen Fessenden, whose husband invented depth sounders as well as wireless radio, proved adept at making the best of awkward living arrangements; she moved her family wherever her husband's work took him and watched as every extra penny was swallowed up by the purchase of new machinery and laboratory equipment. Their story of hardship, however, was not unique. Progress exacted a high toll from most of these inventors and from the people who were close to them.

Apart from personal satisfaction and potential, albeit unlikely, financial success, there was another important reward for inventors in the 19th and early 20th centuries. The public had an almost starstruck respect for those involved in the creation of new technologies; in this scientific golden age, inventors were heroes. History has exaggerated the phenomenon, but for a time, people like Alexander Graham Bell and Thomas Edison were nearly mythic figures, revered and incredibly popular. Science was a fashionable subject, and even an unknown geologist like Abraham Gesner was occasionally able to earn a living by giving public lectures.

Of the inventors included here, some did indeed win lasting prominence and respect. The names Bombardier and Ski-Doo, for instance, are recognized wherever snow falls; others, like Willson, knew fame only during their lifetime, then slipped into the back pages of history; some received little recognition of any kind. Yet all of these people transformed the world so significantly that they remain worthy of our attention today.

These stories teach other lessons as well. They provide insights into the history and nature of invention itself. Inventors are rarely individuals labouring in isolation; they inevitably depend upon the work of those who have gone before. Mabel Bell's Aerial Experiment Association, a group of enthusiasts who were pioneers in the art of aviation, was able to do its finest work because its members were familiar with the theories of Octave Chanute. Georges Desbarats' partner, William Leggo, who based his process of photo-reproduction on the innovations of British photographer Fox Talbot, used the skills passed on to him by his own father, who had studied lithography printing with its inventor, Johann Aloys Senefelder.

The experiences of William Stephenson and Joseph-Armand Bombardier are evidence that the confluence of world events and evolving technology can also have a profound effect on invention. Stephenson invented a machine for transmitting photographs through wires during the intensely productive and technologically innovative period that followed World War I. In a slightly different fashion, Bombardier's well-known Ski-Doo was also a product of the times. It was made possible by the technological developments precipitated by World War II, by which time Bombardier had been waiting years for the production of engines small enough to allow the construction of the kind of machine he envisioned.

Although these biographies are obviously tales of science and investigation, they are also about financial success and failure. Then, as now, invention was a high-stakes game, especially when the time came to attempt commercial development of a new idea. Commercial applications won fortunes for Stephenson and Bombardier and exhausted the wealth of Desbarats and the Aerial Experiment Association. Willson both won and lost fabulous amounts of money at the inventing game, and he did so with staggering ease. Gesner and Fessenden, each in his own way, succeeded in their ambitions but lost out on the rewards, cheated by the interests of sharper business minds.

The power of money all but erased Reginald Fessenden from the history books, and his story explains why sometimes the greatest thinkers and innovators fade into obscurity while lesser figures become famous. Although Fessenden's work forms the very foundation of all modern communications, he is practically unknown, while his contemporary, Guglielmo Marconi, though not an inventor at all, is lauded as the father of radio. The explanation is simple. Marconi gained renown because his name graced a successful and powerful company that benefited from its association with the beginnings of radio. Fessenden, a private citizen, spent a great portion of his life engaged in a legal battle with virtually the whole radio industry, an industry which owed its very existence to him and which thrived by violating his patents.

The repetition of a sad injustice like Fessenden's eventual inadequate court settlement with the Radio Trust of America became increasingly unlikely as the 20th century progressed. Indeed, though Armand Bombardier remained an intriguing exception to the rule, the world of the self-taught, independent inventor was eventually overtaken by the modern practice of research teams working at universities, in government laboratories and in industry. The Aerial Experiment Association's approach to investigation and development proved to be the wave of the future, but the other inventors in this book were a product of the 19th century, which flourished on the ideas and insights generated by people working either in isolation or with a small team of assistants. To a large extent, the romantic image of the inspired genius was eclipsed during the 20th century, supplanted by the implacable reality of research and development programmes and by the coordinated efforts of far-flung centres of inquiry. Willson, Fessenden and Gesner were among the last of a disappearing breed.

The Aerial Experiment Association proved exceptional in another important respect: it was an openly international effort involving both Canadians and Americans, and it conducted its experiments in both Canada and the United States. That feature no doubt owed much to Mabel and Alexander Graham Bell who, in their support of scientific endeavour, demonstrated their firm belief that knowledge should be shared rather than hoarded.

Of course, an international influence has always been a part of

Canadian invention, though it has not always been as benevolent as that of the Bells. Traditionally, Canadian business and finance have been reluctant to support risky new ventures, and inventors have been able to secure backing only by going to the United States or Great Britain. Even Gesner, a descendant of United Empire Loyalists and an ardent nationalist, was eventually forced to leave Canada to find financing in New York City. Of the people treated in this book, in fact, only Bombardier was able to enjoy an entirely homegrown success.

The importance of innovation to domestic industrial development and prosperity is undeniable, and it is worth remembering that good ideas have slipped irretrievably beyond our borders in the past. But this book is not intended to become part of a chorus of national self-criticism. These stories are instead a reminder of the ingenuity and dogged determination that form an integral part of Canadian history.

ABRAHAM GESNER

A BRIGHTER LIGHT

Hard times had hit the Maritime colonies. The end of the War of 1812 had brought a drastic reduction in the British Navy squadron stationed at Halifax, and the community suffered the consequences: farmers could no longer sell their produce as food for the thousands of sailors; shipwrights lost their jobs repairing the great battleships of the North Atlantic; and unneeded lumber began to stockpile as the navy halted orders for new vessels. As the area's major industries faltered, the economy began a long, slow decline. Employment became a luxury, and Abraham Gesner, farmer's son, amateur geologist, budding scientist and the man who would one day help to establish the modern petrochemical industry, turned to one of the world's oldest professions. He decided to become a horse trader.

Travelling from farm to farm, Gesner offered to buy any beast that was destined to be slaughtered from farmers who could no longer afford to feed all of their work animals. Stretching his limited resources, he assembled over 20 horses, which he planned to sell in the West Indies for a handsome profit. Gesner's career promised travel, adventure and financial gain, and the young man set out enthusiastically.

Sailing south along the Eastern Seaboard, one of the world's busiest trade routes in the 18th and 19th centuries, Gesner sold his horses at the first port of call and stayed with the Nova Scotian vessel as it coasted among the tropical islands of the West Indies. By the time he arrived home, however, his pockets held only rock samples and curious souvenirs of the places he had visited.

For his next entrepreneurial adventure, Gesner planned a shorter voyage, one that would require less time and investment and would not be so hard on the animals. After borrowing heavily to buy stock, he sailed again for the south. Once more, with his horses tied in rows on the open deck, Gesner worked as a common seaman. This time, the leisurely trip down the coast ended abruptly in a violent storm near Bermuda. Only the crew survived the shipwreck, and the vessel and cargo disappeared into the foaming waters off Somerset Bay.

Gesner's second ignominious return to Nova Scotia and his third round of buying and horse dealing must have taxed even his stubborn determination. Plagued by debts, he could gather horses only by agreeing to take them on consignment. Before long, he had assembled a small herd, signed aboard the *Mason's Daughter* and set out onto the December seas. Once again, misfortune followed swiftly after him.

The day of departure was full of promise of a fair passage. The ship found favourable winds and made good speed travelling down the Bay of Fundy. Evening found it already approaching the bay's mouth, where the crew prepared to meet the open waters of the North Atlantic. Sails were set, and rigging was checked. Gesner tightened the traces that held his horses in their closely packed rows on the deck.

As the light faded, the winds began to rise and the men made their way carefully across icy decks, cursing as they struggled in the darkness, their hands numb from fumbling with the frozen sheets and halyards. With darkness came a menacing shift in the wind. The familiar rolling of the deck became a dangerous dance underfoot, and the horses began to scream in fear as waves crashed over the bow. Snow blasted across the water, blinding the sailors. As the ship neared the notorious rocks of Brier Island, the crew discovered that the only lighthouse on the whole coast was invisible in the turmoil. The men clung desperately to the rigging and watched powerlessly as the ship began a fatal drift onto the dangerous lee shore. The din of the wind and seas disappeared in the deafening crash of ship's timber on the rocks. The once sturdy, buoyant craft disintegrated, and only with the strength of fear did the crew manage to launch a small boat and make it to shore.

Having survived the sea, however, the crew faced a more serious enemy. Soaked to the skin and exposed to the cold, they could not last long on the open beach. Without warmth, they would die, and yet crew members merely shook their heads when Gesner turned from the water and began to collect firewood. Matches did not yet exist, and the sailors knew the futility of trying to strike a spark with damp flint and tinder. When he had gathered together enough wood and kindling, Gesner pulled a pair of watertight metal boxes from his pockets and soon had a bright fire blazing on the beach. The men huddled near the warmth and survived a cold, miserable night that would otherwise certainly have killed them. In the morning, a fisherman, drawn by the fire and smoke, came ashore and took them to safety.

More than once, Abraham Gesner's love for and study of science delivered him from desperate situations. On that cold December night, he used a trick known only to the trained chemists of his time, a recipe that Gesner had learned during experiments in an old shed behind the family home. In one container were small slivers of wood coated on the end with potassium sulphate and sulphur. He had prepared them himself. When these were dipped into oil of vitriol, which he kept in the other box, and exposed to the air, they burst magically into flame.

Gesner had always been intrigued by the world's minerals that could be burned to produce heat and light. To him, minerals were the earth's gift to humankind, and he was to spend the rest of his life searching for ways to unlock their promise. It was no accident that Abraham Gesner eventually invented kerosene.

Born in 1797, Gesner was the son of a United Empire Loyalist named Henry Gesner who, at the age of 16, had fought with the British in the American Revolution. At the war's end, Henry and his twin brother fled the new republic and settled in the British colony of Nova Scotia, where the government had set aside land for soldiers. There, Henry married Sarah Pineo, a daughter of one of the few French families that had survived the British expulsion of Acadians in the mid-1750s. Together, they settled on land near Cornwallis Dyke, on the west side of the Nova Scotia peninsula, and established a prosperous farm while raising a large family.

According to his grandson, Henry Gesner "believed in no other government but that of God and the King," and he passed on his strong religious convictions to his children, teaching them an implicit faith in the word of the Bible. He had little success, however, in turning his son into a farmer.

The mysteries of the natural world captured Abraham Gesner's imagination at an early age. As a child, he spent hours reading the few books he could get his hands on, and the rest of his time was passed wandering the countryside, collecting rocks and other curiosities. His father wisely forgave him his shortcomings as a farmer's son and encouraged the boy's studies, arranging for what education he could and even going so far as to convert an old shed on the family property into a laboratory in which Abraham conducted his occasionally explosive and often evil-smelling experiments. In that shack, young Gesner learned to make the matches that later saved his life on the cold shores of Brier Island.

As a young man, Gesner had the good fortune to befriend Bill Webster, the son of a local doctor. Bill was to be much more than simply Gesner's companion on his explorations of the countryside. Since doctors in the 19th century prepared their own medicines, working with burners and beakers and a mortar and pestle to grind powders, Bill's father's small pharmacy probably provided the future scientist with his first taste of chemistry and set him on the path that he was to follow all his life. But there was another member of the Webster family who would prove even more significant in Gesner's life — Bill's sister Harriet. Although she came from a family of some means, Harriet Webster had little time for social pretensions, preferring the company of her brother and his intense young friend. Not only did she appreciate Gesner's love of science and understand his enthusiasm for the secrets of the natural world, but she also shared his love of music. The pair would create an evening's entertainment, with Gesner accompanying Harriet on his flute as she played the piano.

DR. ABRAHAM GESNER

In spite of his unconventional ways and the failure of his early horse-trading ventures, Harriet married Gesner only a few months after the last of his ill-fated trips. Although Gesner was filled with wonderful plans and ideas, he appeared unable to bring them to fruition; in marrying him, Harriet was taking a considerable risk. Gesner already had several debts, which increased over the next year. Yet their relationship endured, and throughout what was to be Gesner's long and varied career, Harriet provided a stable centre, raising their family, encouraging her husband, discussing his work and helping him shape his research into theories.

Nonetheless, the early years were difficult. When Gesner faced debtor's prison, his father-in-law made him an offer he found impossible to turn down. While he refused to pay off the young man's creditors, the elder Webster would provide the means for Gesner to avoid jail by immigrating to England to attend medical school. That time proved to be the most miserable period of Gesner's life. It would be another 40 years before Dr. Joseph Lister introduced the notion of antiseptic techniques into hospitals, and the institutions Gesner attended were filthy places where disease and death ran rampant. Raised in the open countryside of Nova Scotia, he could not adjust to London's cramped and seething streets. He longed for his home and the vigorous outdoor life he knew best. He suffered the condescension and scorn of other students who considered anyone from distant Nova Scotia an uncivilized "colonial." And he missed his wife and infant son.

Gesner seemed an unlikely candidate for a career in medicine, believing as he did that disease and death were simply another aspect of the divine plan and that treatment directly interfered with God's will. Yet he possessed the necessary skills and mastered his subjects with relative ease. Medical schools of the day did not assign a timetable; students merely attended lectures and did rounds with an instructing doctor. They progressed as quickly as they could master each subject, and Gesner, no doubt, devoted himself to his studies, knowing that the faster he learned, the sooner he would be home.

After spending his first six months at Guy's Hospital, Gesner moved on to St. Bartholomew's for intensive anatomy training and instruction in surgery. He spent gloomy days in the dissecting rooms, and although he no longer faced daily rounds in hospital wards filled with suffering and death, the unpreserved corpses gave off a suffocating stench that clung mercilessly to the students' clothes, hair and skin.

At St. Bartholomew's, Gesner came under the influence of Dr. John Abernathy, a famed lecturer of the day and a terrifying little man with a reputation for intimidating students and patients alike with his eccentric ways. Abernathy did not suffer fools kindly and had little sympathy for patients who he believed had caused their own problems by intemperance or for students whose ambitions exceeded their talents. In Gesner, however, he recognized a kindred spirit, for as well as teaching medicine, Abernathy dabbled in the sciences. He kept a small laboratory in his home and considered himself an accomplished chemist. When Abernathy became aware that the rough young colonial in his classes was a self-taught chemist of some skill, he invited Gesner to join a group of scientists to which he belonged. Abernathy's discerning assessment of Gesner's talent marked a turning point in the younger man's life. The regular meetings brought some pleasure into Gesner's bleak London existence. Members of the group listened with rapt attention as he described the geological and mineralogical wonders of the distant colony, telling stories of beaches strewn with semiprecious stones and of 40-foot tides that swept whole rivers back upon themselves. He discussed the geological mysteries that had puzzled him since his youth and heard advice from Charles Lyell, a London lawyer destined to become one of the world's most important early geologists. In short, the meetings introduced Gesner to the world of contemporary science. He met leading scientists with whom he would correspond for the rest of his life. Beyond the invaluable education he gained in their presence, he learned that here was a place he belonged, where he commanded respect and could make a contribution.

The pleasure of those meetings, however, as well as his medical education, came to an abrupt end with the news from Nova Scotia that his young son had died. Abernathy, learning of his friend's situation, signed the final papers qualifying Gesner as a medical doctor, and almost overnight, the exile in London ended and Gesner found himself heading across the North Atlantic for Canada.

Good fortune had led Gesner to John Abernathy, and Abernathy and the others of his scientific club gave Gesner the confidence to pursue his own investigations. But it was Gesner's own unquenchable spirit and his capacity for work that eventually established him among the ranks of the world's first geologists. When he set up his practice as a doctor in 1827, Gesner chose the village of Parrsboro, Nova Scotia, more for its terrain than for its medical prospects. While on his country rounds, he hunted far more eagerly for interesting geological specimens than for new patients.

To Gesner, the medical profession was a source of income rather than a calling. His cheerful eloquence and the news of the world that he brought to his patients may have been a comfort, but he felt the frustration of rarely being able to offer a cure for the suffering he saw. Instead, he gave his attention to the study of geology. He read every book he could find on the subject, and he applied what he learned to the land around him. He corresponded with scientists around the world, seeking advice and offering opinions. And within the space of a few years, he had acquired an enviable education and a broad measure of practical expertise. Only nine years after settling in Parrsboro, he published a 300-page treatise entitled *Remarks on the Geology and Mineralogy of Nova Scotia*. Patterned very loosely on *The Geology of Nova Scotia*, an essay by American geologists Francis Alger and Charles Jackson, Gesner displayed not only the breadth of his knowledge but also a deceptively simple and engaging prose style that won him a wide audience. He reduced theories to their essences and emphasized the practical applications of his theories and discoveries, pointing the way toward commercial development of the colony's resources.

In the years at Parrsboro, he also began the long journeys of wilder-

A SMALL PART OF THE GESNER COLLECTION

ness exploration that provided the material for his books and theories, and he accepted regular invitations to give lectures on scientific progress and on the technological novelties of the age. Everywhere he went, he made careful observations and took copious notes. Like his London anatomy professors mapping the human body, Gesner searched for evidence that would show him the form of the great sleeping skeleton of stone which lay beneath the colony's cultivated fields and endless living wilderness.

Although Gesner's early understanding of geology and many of the leading theories he relied on became obsolete within his lifetime, his work constituted a well-informed and sophisticated contribution to the emerging science of the time, and his fieldwork, maps and plottings of geological formations laid an essential foundation for all subsequent work in Nova Scotia and New Brunswick.

His experience was typical of an age in which science remained tightly bound by religious dogma, and Gesner himself accepted biblical references as grounds for his theories. He attempted to explain geological phenomena, for instance, by reference to Noah's flood. But after calculating that 40 days and 40 nights of rain would not have produced sufficient water to shape the surface of the planet, he hypothesized that an earlier deluge had covered the earth to much greater depths and had shaped the face of lands as they emerged from the floodwater seas. Left out of the hypothesis, however, was the impact of the earth's last Ice Age, when silent walls of ice, miles thick, pushed down over the continents and carved a new face in the earth's surface.

For all the unavoidable theoretical errors of his age, Gesner nonetheless compiled an invaluable store of empirical information that made him unique in the eastern colonies of British North America. As a result, the release of his first book in 1836 established his reputation as a knowledgeable geologist. It attracted businessmen and mining speculators and, most importantly, freed him from what he viewed as the drudgery of the medical profession.

In 1837, he set off to explore the St. Croix River Valley and Charlotte County, New Brunswick, for a private company interested in locating new coal deposits. A year later, he accepted a government-paid position as geologist for New Brunswick and moved his family to Saint John. For five years, he crisscrossed the province, gathering data for a geological map, assembling samples and labouring to piece together a comprehensive picture of the colony. Each summer, he travelled into new regions, collecting anything that piqued his insatiable curiosity — rocks, plants and animals alike. Each winter, he wrote public reports on his findings and catalogued his growing collection of natural curios, practising his taxidermy skills in order to preserve samples of the wildlife he encountered.

The years of alternate travel and writing were a happy time for Gesner, exciting but secure. Ironically, though, it was the optimism that he felt and reflected in his reports which brought to an end his tenure as official geologist. Although his exhaustive observations could not be faulted, his effusive claims about the possibility of developing various mineral deposits did not take into account the cost of refining low-grade ore or the expense of transportation from remote regions. When companies that had been formed to exploit Gesner's discoveries went bankrupt, Gesner himself was held responsible for their failure. In reaction, the government refused to pay either his salary or his travel costs for 1841 and 1842, and Gesner was once more in financial difficulty.

Although the issue involved Gesner in years of lawsuits and interfered with his work on the geological map of New Brunswick, he was not discouraged for long. He took on other assignments, including a survey of Prince Edward Island in 1846, and he opened a museum to display the thousands of artifacts he had collected that now overflowed his house and were taking up rented space. Unfortunately, the museum also failed, and Gesner's kindhearted creditors — friends and men who respected his work — accepted the collection in place of payment. In turn, they donated the collection intact to the Mechanics' Institute, and eventually, many of Gesner's pieces formed part of the foundation of the New Brunswick Museum of Saint John.

Good fortune, in fact, smiled on the world when Abraham Gesner lost his government post. Although the dismissal meant renewed economic woes for his family, it led Gesner back to the laboratory, where he resumed a line of inquiry that had first occurred to him when, as an ill-fated young horse trader, he had looked out over the famous lake of pitch on the Caribbean island of Trinidad. More than three miles wide and filled with a thick, sticky tar, the immense deposit and the possibilities it held still stirred Gesner's imagination. Back in Cornwallis, Nova Scotia, medicine once more provided an income, while science filled Gesner's evenings with dreams and inspiration. He experimented with the newfound wonders of galvanism, as electricity was then called, and he designed a small motor that was a forerunner of the dynamo,

THE MECHANICS' INSTITUTE, SAINT JOHN, NEW BRUNSWICK, CIRCA 1900

a machine capable of converting mechanical energy into direct electric current. Because prepared insulated wire did not yet exist, Gesner also invented a machine that wrapped a tight insulating sleeve of yarn around a bare metal core.

His forays into gadgetry, however, did not distract him from his examinations of coal and oil and other related hydrocarbons. He found a means of compressing coal dust into even-burning briquets; he experimented with wood preservatives and paving asphalt; and at last, Gesner discovered the process for distilling lamp oil from bitumen. More importantly, he perfected the appliances required for distillation. He cleared away the remaining technical obstacles and established beyond any doubt that the filthy blackness of coal and petroleum sands and shale could be transformed into a clean, white, bright-burning lamp oil.

In the first half of the 19th century, providing light for the evening hours was a costly, dirty and even dangerous business. Wood and coal could be burned for satisfactory heat, but the so-called illuminants of the day provided only a dim yellow light, barely sufficient to read by and scarcely an improvement on the open-hearth fires that humans had depended on for hundreds of years. Candles, oils from whales, fish, seals, rapeseed, even rushes and splints of lard burned in a saucer — these provided the only alternatives to total darkness once the sun went down. Strangely enough, most illuminants were edible products. People lit their homes with foodstuffs, and the substances commonly in use produced a greasy smoke as well as an odour.

One product used for many years avoided some of these problems but also introduced the constant threat of fire and explosion. "Burning fluid," as it was known, produced a bright flame and relatively little smoke, but as it was composed of equal parts of turpentine and alcohol, any lamp filled with the substance was a potential bomb burning cheerily in its wall sconce or on a bedside table.

By 1850, whale oil, considered by many to be the finest illuminant and also widely used as a lubricant, rose dramatically in price as the great mammals became rare and whalers had to search farther to fill the holds of their ships. The extravagant prices encouraged a widespread effort to find a substitute, and it was common knowledge that the discoverer of an alternative illuminant would become very wealthy indeed.

Although his invention of kerosene had a far-reaching impact, Gesner made no record of the precise date on which he perfected his process for distilling lamp oil from coal. In his years as the New Brunswick colonial geologist, he also began giving popular lectures in which he described advances in the world of science and technology. Entranced audiences heard his descriptions of the geological skeleton of the world and listened as he explained the unfolding wonders of galvanism. As often as not, Gesner simply talked of his own latest interest and presented the results of experiments he had tried. With an enthusiasm that always won over his audience, he wove dry technical details into magical tales of progress. An advertised talk by Dr. Gesner always drew a full crowd, and it was at a lecture in Prince Edward Island in August 1846 that he first introduced the substance he called "keroselain," a word derived from the Greek for "wax oil." He ended a talk on heat by lighting a lamp filled with his new oil. In a crowd of people long used to the dingy light and smoke produced by the lamp oils of the day, Gesner's demonstration must have caused a sensation.

Burning with a brilliant light, the kerosene (as it was later renamed) gave off almost no smoke at all.

While Gesner's lectures were a success, little attention was given to the remarkable oil. It seemed only a curiosity. Gesner knew that without better raw materials than those he had available, the oil would remain a novelty, too expensive to produce commercially.

By the time he applied for a patent eight years later, however, Gesner was able to describe the perfected process. The application leaves no doubt about the means he used to extract his lamp oil. In clear, simple language, he set forth the steps for distillation and purification. Gesner, in fact, distinguished three grades of kerosene: A, B and C. The first two would become familiar to later experts as the light and heavy fractions of gasoline. For Gesner's purposes, they were too dangerously volatile. But the third was a miraculous success. It burned with a bright yellow light and could be handled safely. It gave off little odour, and beyond its use as an illuminant, it had good lubricating properties.

That advantage alone would have guaranteed its success had kerosene failed as a lamp oil. Since the first days of the industrial revolution, engineers had looked for effective ways of greasing and cooling the whirling gears and shafts of steam-driven machinery. The incredible speed of the new steam looms and presses and the heat from friction they produced quickly broke down the fats and natural organic oils traditionally used for lubrication. In the midst of headlong industrial development, new technologies often foundered for lack of good-quality lubricants, and coal oils provided a long-awaited and desperately needed solution.

The production of oil from raw coal began with distillation in a closed retort. Coal was broken into chunks and heated over a carefully controlled flame, and the vapours rising out of the black mineral passed into a condensing tube fixed to the top of the container. Liquids driven from the coal by heating flowed directly into a tank, and as the vapours condensed into a fluid, they, too, passed into the same container.

The combined product of that first distillation was left undisturbed for several hours so that any water in the mixture would settle to the bottom of the tank along with solid impurities. After roughly 12 hours, Gesner drew off the oil.

Following the careful work of distillation, kerosene C had to be treated to remove the additional impurities that caused smoke and gave the raw substance its pungent smell. Sulphuric acid was added to the oil, and they were thoroughly mixed, then left to settle for another 12 hours. The acid combined with any tars still present, and again, a heavy sludge settled out of the solution. In order to neutralize the remaining acid, Gesner added calcined lime, which also served to absorb any remaining traces of water. One last distilling gave Gesner his final product — purified kerosene. According to an advertisement circulated at the time, the sensational new oil produced "the cheapest and most brilliant light ever" and gave "a light equal to three burning fluid lamps of two wicks each at half the cost."

Although the first beaker of kerosene was a glorious victory, Gesner had also unearthed a cornucopia of other products made from coal and other natural bituminous tars. By the time he acquired his American patents, Gesner had thoroughly examined the by-products of the cleansing process. Depending on its particular composition, a bituminous material would provide not only light but also a variety of quite different saleable goods. The company eventually formed to exploit Gesner's patents circulated pamphlets predicting that it would someday supply not only the new kerosene but also solvents, waterproofing, paving material, electrical-wire insulation, railway grease and even paints and varnishes, each made from the distillate of dry coal.

The son of a staunch British Loyalist, Gesner often displayed a strong nationalism. It appears doubly strange, then, that he took his discovery to the United States for development. But his bitterness over a questionable court decision in Nova Scotia and the timidity of local investors probably account for his decision. In any case, he moved his family to New York, secured his 1854 patents for the distillation process and sold the rights to a group of wealthy developers who, with Gesner's guidance in the design of the refinery and services as company chemist, launched a spectacularly prosperous enterprise.

In less than two years, the North American Kerosene Gas Light Company began to generate a handsome profit for its investors. Kerosene became the most successful lamp oil ever produced, but the factory Gesner designed in New York City demonstrated something far more important. The simplicity and ingenuity of his original refinery helped prove that a wealth of useful materials could be extracted from hydrocarbons (coal and asphalt and, later, oil) by a careful succession of chemical treatments and repeated distillation. The single New York factory set in motion a series of advances that led directly to the development of oil drilling and the establishment of the entire petrochemical

ABRAHAM
CESNER,
M.D., F.C.S.
GEOLOGIST
BORN AT
CORNWALLIS, N.S.
MAY 2, 1797,
DIED AT HALIFAX
APRIL 29, 1864.

HIS TREATISE ON
THE GEOLOGY AND
MINERALOGY OF
NOVA SCOTIA, 1856
WAS ONE OF THE
EARLIEST WORKS
DEALING WITH THOSE
SUBJECTS IN THIS
PROVINCE AND ABOUT
1852 HE WAS THE
AMERICAN INVENTOR
OF THE PROCESS OF
KEROSENE OIL

ERECTED BY
IMPERIAL OIL LTD.
AS A TOKEN OF
APPRECIATION AND
FOR HIS IMPORTANT
CONTRIBUTION TO
THE OIL INDUSTRY.

GESNER

"ERECTED BY IMPERIAL OIL LTD. AS A TOKEN OF APPRECIATION . . ." 1933 industry. Oil originally served simply as a raw-material substitute for coal, and the essentials of modern refining can all be found in the technology that Gesner designed for the New York plant.

Never much of a businessman, Gesner had done little to secure his place within the enterprise he had made possible, and in the late 1850s, he was released from his position as company chemist. The company continued to thrive for several years and survived a number of owners, eventually ending up as part of J.D. Rockefeller's Standard Oil. Gesner was forced once more to return to the medical profession to earn a living. The family remained in New York, and Gesner again picked up his pen, writing a book called *A Practical Treatise on Coal, Petroleum and Other Distilled Oils*, which remained a standard text for the industry for several decades. In 1864, at the age of 67, the geologist, affectionately called "Wise Man" by the Micmac natives who accompanied him on his numerous explorations, died of a heart attack.

Sixty-nine years after Abraham Gesner's death, Imperial Oil placed a monument at his grave in recognition of the Nova Scotian's essential role in shaping not only the refining industry but also the course of the 20th century. Gesner's skills as a geologist and a chemist created a product destined to light the evening darkness of millions of homes across North America; and his refinery designs achieved such efficiency that they were copied by other companies for decades to come, even after petroleum had replaced coal as a raw material. Where trained scientists, chemists and engineers had failed, the medical doctor from Nova Scotia succeeded. A lifetime of study had finally enabled Gesner to interpret the natural secrets that had tantalized him since the earliest days of his childhood.

SANDFORD FLEMING

SETTING THE WORLD'S WATCH

On a clear July day in 1858, Sandford Fleming missed his train at Nottawasaga, a small town 60 miles north of Toronto. As chief engineer of the nearly completed Ontario, Simcoe and Huron Railway, he had urgent business in the city. Thinking that he might catch up to the train when it stopped at Barrie, he set out on foot along the tracks that had so recently been laid by his crews. Fleming found himself walking through the northern woods armed with only an umbrella, keeping his head down as he stepped quickly from one tie to the next.

Having surveyed the line and then supervised its construction, Fleming was familiar with every foot of the route he was travelling. He paid little attention as the forest on either side of the track gave way to swampland. It was not until he was overtaken by an eerie sense that he was being watched that he looked up. There, sitting peacefully in the middle of the track, sat a large bear. The animal seemed content on the dry, sunny ridge that Fleming's railway crews had built in the middle of the forest, and it gave no indication that it was prepared to move.

Fleming pulled himself up with a start. As he worked to control his initial fear, he began almost immediately to fume at the delay, cursing the obstructing brute. He looked behind him and into the oozing marsh on either side of the track. He thought again of the meetings awaiting him in Toronto and, after a moment's pause, decided that he had no option. Staring intently at the bear, he abandoned discretion and rallied all the valour he possessed. Raising his umbrella high, he ran screaming toward the animal.

Whether the bear was simply taken by surprise or whether it was offended by Fleming's rude greeting, it clambered to its feet and ran off into the swamp. No doubt pleased and more than a little relieved, Fleming carried on and caught his train just as it pulled out of the Barrie station.

Throughout his life, Sandford Fleming faced each problem with just such a combination of imagination and forthright determination. He possessed boundless energy and an utterly tenacious sense of purpose and was apparently rarely discouraged either by setbacks or by the shortsightedness of others. By the time of his death in 1915, Sir Sandford Fleming was one of the most respected engineers in Canada. He had founded what is today known as the Royal Canadian Institute, a society dedicated to the recognition and encouragement of the arts and sciences in Canada, and served as the chancellor of Queen's University at Kingston, Ontario, for 35 years. He had been the persistent advocate of an underwater cable linking Canada and Australia, which he believed was the solution to the communication problem facing the far-flung colonies of the British Empire. But two of the greatest achievements of his long and illustrious career — masterminding the construction of a railway line that spanned the new nation of Canada and devising an internationally recognized system of timekeeping — are even more eloquent testaments to his resolute vision.

THE YOUNG IMMIGRANT, 1845

Born in Kirkcaldy, Scotland, in 1827, Sandford Fleming left his home at the age of 18 and, with his brother David, sailed for the New World. Their Atlantic crossing was so rough that at one point, the young Flemings composed a farewell letter to their family and threw it overboard sealed in a bottle. Sandford arrived in Canada trained to work as a draftsman and a surveyor, while his elder brother was skilled as a carpenter and woodworker. Armed with letters of introduction, Sandford enthusiastically set about establishing himself in the British colonies of North America.

While David found work immediately after the pair had arrived in Toronto, Sandford spent fruitless days searching for employment and hearing discouraging news from the people who he had been told could help him. After 2½ months in the country, the glorious career he sought in the New World still eluded him. Fleming was warned by Dr. John Strachan, then bishop of Toronto, that the country's great works had all been completed and that the colony no longer required men with Fleming's training. The system of canals that linked Ottawa, or Bytown, as it was then known, with the Great Lakes was already in operation, and the cities had been laid out. Toronto, with 20,000 inhabitants, had gas lighting and its own waterworks, and roads had been carved into the wilderness where settlers toiled to turn the forests into farmland. The heyday of the engineers, according to Strachan, had passed.

Casimir Gzowski, the head of the Department of Roads and Harbours, likewise assured young Fleming that there was no work to be had in the whole of the province, that funds were exhausted and engineers were being laid off. Gzowski ended their disheartening meeting by advising Fleming to return to Scotland, where the prospects for a professional man were, no doubt, far better. For weeks on end, Fleming heard the same advice echoed by others.

Undaunted by that bleak picture, Fleming set about carving out a place for himself by acquiring the experience and education he needed to become a full-fledged land surveyor. Finding himself short of money, he surveyed several Ontario towns and drew up the first maps of Peterborough, Newcastle and Cobourg, among others. These he planned to sell, and when he was unable to find a lithographer, he gathered together the equipment he needed and produced the maps himself, eventually selling hundreds of copies as he travelled around southeastern Ontario. At the same time, he began to produce engravings of municipal buildings and scenes of activities in the towns and cities. Encouraged by his success, Fleming even undertook the mapping of the city of Toronto, including soundings of the harbour taken from a boat and through holes drilled in the winter ice.

Although he was colour-blind — he reportedly once painted a landscape with bright red lawns — Fleming's talents with pen and ink earned him a considerable reputation during his early years in Toronto. In fact, Sandford Fleming was the first to use the beaver as a Canadian symbol as he designed the famous threepenny beaver postage stamp, issued on April 23, 1851. Not only was the threepenny the first stamp issued in Canada, but it was also among the earliest pictorial stamps in the world. Until then, only numerals or a representation of a country's monarch had adorned the royal mails.

After months of study, Fleming travelled to Montreal — then the seat of government — to take his surveying examinations. Despite the pessimistic predictions of Strachan and Gzowski, there was indeed interesting work for a man with the right qualifications, and Fleming intended to be involved. On April 25, 1849, after successfully completing two days of tests and interviews and armed with his commission from the governor as a land surveyor, he stepped out onto the streets of Montreal ready to take up his career in earnest. By a fluke of circumstance, he also stepped out into the midst of the Montreal Riots.

Following the passage in Parliament that same day of the Rebellion

FLEMING'S THREEPENNY BEAVER, FIRST CANADIAN POSTAGE STAMP, 1851

Losses Bill, angry speeches filled the air of the Champ de Mars, a public square in old Montreal. The noise of the crowd and the impassioned oratory attracted Fleming's attention. When someone yelled out, "Burn the Parliament building," the mob rushed off bearing torches through the narrow streets, and Fleming followed along to witness the spectacle. Years later, he set down his own account of what followed, revealing his strong loyalty as a citizen of the British Empire:

"When they reached the building, they tore up the planks of the sidewalk and dashed them through the lower windows. Lights were then applied to piles of parliamentary papers inside by throwing in the torches. The fire spread rapidly, and I could see that before long, it would reach the library. Having spent several delightful days there examining old and rare books, I felt that the least I could do was to try to save some of them. I gained an entrance but found that the fire had already taken possession of the library, and it was impossible to do anything there. Turning to the legislative hall, I saw the Queen's picture and determined to make at least an effort to save it. Three other men

BUILDING THE INTERCOLONIAL RAILWAY, 1870 (FLEMING IN TOP HAT)

joined me, but we found it no easy task. The portrait was in a massive gilt frame, firmly bolted to the wall. At last, by putting our shoulders underneath and exerting our united strength, we managed to loosen the fastenings, and finally the frame came down with a crash. Finding the frame too heavy to handle, we removed the canvas on its stretching frame, and the four of us carried it out of the building, a shoulder under each corner. We were only just in time, for as we climbed slowly down the stairs, the flames were roaring overhead, and we had to stoop low to prevent the picture being scorched. The picture was removed to a place of safety and, some years after, was brought to Ottawa. It hangs today in the Senate. . . ."

The years surrounding the Confederation of the Dominion of Canada were filled with demands for transportation facilities to link the scattered colonies of British North America; that meant establishing a rail system which could span the continent. The immense challenge included unparallelled difficulties. Indeed, Strachan's claim that everything of value in the colonies had already been completed couldn't have been further from the truth. From the east coast to the settled areas of Upper Canada, the tracks had to be laid through hundreds of miles of often untouched forests. More than 30 major bridges had to be built, and a tunnel 166 feet long had to be cut through Morrissey's Rock, near Campbellton, New Brunswick. Farther west, more dense forests and the tumbled rock of the Precambrian Shield stretched away to the north. Beyond lay thousands of miles of open prairie and then the western mountains rising up like a wall and blocking passage to the coast.

Here were projects large enough to absorb even Sandford Fleming's vast imagination and energies, and he plunged into the task of stitching the country together with railroads — a task that occupied the next 35 years of his life. He began as one of two assistant engineers of the Ontario, Simcoe and Huron line in 1852, then became chief engineer of its successor line, the Northern, in 1857. In 1860, with most of the track already completed, he personally escorted the royal party of the Prince of Wales over what was then the longest track in the British North American colonies.

In 1863, as Fleming worked to enlist support for a transcontinental line, the government decided to build a railroad that would connect Upper and Lower Canada with the Maritime colonies of New Brunswick and Nova Scotia. Since the cost of the project was to be shared by the British government, the united Canadas and the Maritime governments, a three-man commission was set up to oversee the survey of the line, and Fleming was chosen as the Canadian representative. He was also chosen by New Brunswick and Nova Scotia to be their commissioner, and in a third independent decision, the colonial secretary in London announced that he wished Fleming to serve as the imperial representative as well. This remarkable coincidence reflected an overall trust and confidence in Sandford Fleming's ability to oversee the construction of an entire railroad. He began immediately, and the middle of the winter of 1864 found him and his companions making their way across the Gaspé Peninsula on snowshoes, walking over the proposed routes and making preliminary surveys.

After laying down the route, Fleming was appointed chief engineer and spent 13 years supervising the construction of what came to be known as the Intercolonial Railway. He included the widespread use of iron bridges in his plans, arguing that such bridges not only would stand up to wear better than wooden trusses but also would be free from the common risk of fires ignited by sparks from passing locomotives. He defended his radical decision against stiff opposition. Many, including the board of governors appointed to oversee the project, claimed that the iron beams would crack under the weight of a loaded train, and they withheld their approval even after the construction of several of the bridges was complete. Fleming eventually laid the argument to rest by inviting the governors to a lunch that he ordered served *under* one of the controversial spans. As the meal got under way, a train pulled out onto the bridge and made its way to the other side. Fleming continued with his meal undisturbed, but the others sat in horror as the train continued to shunt back and forth. The bridge, however, stood in silence above them, neither swaying nor creaking. Fleming had made his point. He was left to finish the remaining bridges without interference.

Before the Intercolonial was completed in the summer of 1876, the government decided to begin work on the vast Canadian Pacific Railway (CPR) line, intended to run from Montreal to the Pacific Coast. Deemed the most qualified man in the country, Fleming was asked to head the survey for this line as well, and although he had dreamed of such a project for years, he decided that he could not manage the added responsibilities. The government refused to accept his decision, however, and despite his best efforts to the contrary, Fleming found himself in control of not one but two railroads — two lines that would eventually join and cross the continent.

In 1872, as 10,000 men continued to labour to complete the tracks for the Intercolonial, Fleming once again set out into the wilderness to gain an overview of a survey route, this time making a three-month trek west across the continent. Fleming's exploration party included his son Frank as well as a doctor, a botanist, a minister and several others. While they planned the route for a railroad that would someday whisk people across the country in comfort, their trip was made slowly over rugged terrain. They travelled in canoes that were alternately towed by tiny steamers plying the northern lakes and paddled by native guides. They rode in wagons and Red River carts, on horses and mules and often went on foot. Food for much of the journey was pemmican, and at night, they slept in tents, except on those rare occasions when they stayed at one of the Hudson's Bay Company's settlements scattered across the west. Conditions were often primitive, and at times, supplies had to be rationed; but by the time they reached

THE CANADIAN PACIFIC RAILWAY SURVEY, 1871-1872

the west coast, they had not only established the most viable survey lines but had also done extensive informal botanical and geological research, carefully examining the prospects for settlement in each of the areas they had encountered.

After the initial survey, the government abandoned its plans to finance the CPR, and although Fleming became part of the private company that was formed to carry on the work, he did not act as chief engineer. Ten years later, however, with progress stalled at the foot of the mountains, he was summoned once again and asked to find a new route through the Selkirk Mountains, a range west of Calgary, well south of the line he had originally proposed. Returning from England in 1883 to make the trip, he once again took to the trail after travelling across much of the continent on the route he had laid out a decade before. This time, he and his companions almost starved to death in the wilderness when their rendezvous with a supply party from the west coast was delayed. But in the end, their survey of Rogers Pass cleared the way for construction crews to hook up with lines being built from the west. The railroad that Fleming had dreamed of in the 1850s finally spanned the continent in 1885, and he is pictured among the dignitaries and workers in the famous photograph of the last spike being driven at Craigellachie, British Columbia.

Perhaps Fleming's most valuable asset was his talent for spotting a simple solution to a problem whose inconvenience others had long tolerated. It is not surprising, then, that the second achievement for which he is acclaimed — the international adoption of Standard Time — began with a seemingly trivial incident. Held up at a train station in Ireland for over 16 hours by a typographical confusion between 5:35 a.m. and 5:35 p.m., Fleming began to consider ways of improving the contemporary system of time measurement. He made a thorough study of the different methods used around the world and throughout history, examining ways of marking off the hours and researching means of coping with the varying length of daylight throughout the year. He confronted the problem of the earth's rotation — the different positions relative to the sun of points around the globe. In a paper he prepared for private circulation, he described the incredible variety of systems available:

"The Italians, the Bohemians and the Poles have a division of the day into 24 parts, numbered from the first to the twenty-fourth — from one o'clock to twenty-four o'clock. . . . In Japan, there are four principal points of division — noon, midnight, sunset and sunrise — dividing the natural day into four variable parts. These four parts are each divided into three equal portions, together making 12 hours. Each hour is again divided into 12 parts, thus making in all 144 subdivisions of the day. . . . The day is reckoned to begin in China before midnight, the first hour extending from 11 p.m. to 1 a.m. by our mode of reckoning. The Jews, Turks, Austrians and others, with some of the Italians, have begun their day at sunset. The Arabians begin their day at noon. . . . The ancient Egyptians divided the day equally into day and night and again subdivided each half into 12 hours, numbered from 1 to 12; the night with them commenced six hours before and terminated six hours after midnight; the day began six hours before noon and lasted 12 hours, or until six hours after noon. . . . The common practice at present with most civilized nations is to divide the day into two series of 12 hours each, a custom which corresponds very closely to that followed by the ancient Egyptians long before the Christian era. Thus while we have made extraordinary advances in all the arts and

SIR SANDFORD FLEMING, 1895, CHANCELLOR OF QUEEN'S UNIVERSITY

sciences and in their application to everyday life, we find ourselves cling-
ing to a conventional and inconvenient mode of computing time, one
not materially different from that practised by the Egyptians perhaps
30 centuries ago."

Although Fleming quickly realized that the problem of confusing
a.m. and p.m. could be easily solved by adopting the 24-hour clock,
he had by then also identified other serious problems, and he soon
became a central figure in the international push to work out solutions.
In the modern age of rapid transportation by rail and communication
by telegraph, the differences between local times in different cities
threatened to make scheduling a chaotic venture, and in North America, the problem was especially acute. Inhabitants of the Maritimes and
the Eastern Seaboard were four or five full hours into the day before
the sun rose on the west coast of the continent, and in between these
two extremes, every city and town set its clocks differently according
to its position relative to the sun. Frequent travellers carried watches
with several faces, each set to a local standard; and to complete the con-

fusion, the railroads had to maintain their own systems in order to make scheduling possible. A train passing through five cities might be carrying timepieces with up to six entirely different and unrelated settings. And each of them would be correct.

"To illustrate the points of difficulty," Fleming wrote in 1876, "let us first take the case of a traveller in North America. He lands, let us say, at Halifax, in Nova Scotia, and starts on a railway journey through the eastern portions of Canada. His route is over the Intercolonial and Grand Trunk lines. He stops at Saint John, Quebec, Montreal, Ottawa and Toronto. At the beginning of the journey, he sets his watch by Halifax time. As he reaches each place in succession, he finds a considerable variation in the clocks by which the trains are run, and he discovers that at no two places is the same time used. Between Halifax and Toronto, he finds the railways employing no fewer than five different standards of time. If the traveller remained at any one of the cities referred to, he would be obliged to alter his watch in order to avoid much inconvenience and perhaps not a few disappointments and annoyances to himself and others. If, however, he should not alter his watch, he would discover on reaching Toronto that it was an hour and five minutes faster than the clocks and watches in the city."

Describing a trip from England to India, Fleming pointed out that the problem would eventually become even more serious on a global scale; between England and China, a traveller's watch would fall behind by more than eight hours. Clearly, any solution he proposed would have to be international in scope.

Because the earth rotates, sunlight appears to sweep around the globe, lighting first one area and then the next. It takes one full day for every line of longitude to pass under the sun, and if one travels east or west, the sun will be seen directly overhead (the position at 12 o'clock noon) at a different time. Before standard time, this meant that every city slightly to the west of another would have to set its clocks a few minutes behind. And although each setting would reflect the position of the sun at noon, there would be no relation between them.

As long as people carried out most of their daily activities in one locality, the differences did not matter. Farm communities experienced no confusion, and a person travelling for a day by foot or on horseback rarely encountered a problem. With improvements to transportation, however, people covered increasing distances with greater and greater ease. The North American network of railway lines grew larger with every week that passed. Thousands of miles of new track were being laid, and along with the benefits came the kind of chaos that Fleming had presented in his description of the train ride from Halifax to Toronto. Time reckoning had become a uniquely modern problem. Fleming insisted that it required a modern solution.

As an answer, Fleming originally suggested creating what he called "Terrestrial Time," a 24-hour system that substituted the numbers 13 to 24 for the hours of the afternoon and evening. Two p.m. in Terrestrial Time, he explained, would become 14 o'clock, and 7 p.m. would be known as 19 o'clock. No two hours in the day would be designated by the same number, and the confusion between a.m. and p.m. — which first drew Fleming's attention to the issue of timekeeping — would be avoided. To address the problem of differing local times, Fleming also proposed that Terrestrial Time should be the same throughout the world. No matter where the sun was in the sky, the Terrestrial clock at any location would be at the same setting as it was everywhere else. When it was 15 o'clock in Halifax, it would also be 15 o'clock in Rome and Calcutta and Singapore. Local time, he argued, could still be reckoned according to the position of the sun, but for the important scheduling of navigation and commerce, Terrestrial Time clocks would be identical around the globe.

After circulating his ideas in a private pamphlet, Fleming approached the British Association for the Advancement of Science and was invited to present his plan at their 1878 conference. But after crossing the Atlantic to Dublin, Ireland, and waiting patiently through several days of presentations, he was told that his ideas did not merit consideration. Given no opportunity to speak, he returned to Canada disappointed but also angered at the association's lack of foresight.

Undaunted, however, Fleming noted upon his return to North America that "in the Chicago newspapers was the notice of a meeting of the railway managers of the United States and Canada to take definite action on the subject of regulating time." Encouraged by the attention being paid to the railway-scheduling chaos, he determined to press on, observing with smug satisfaction that "the British Association . . . itself was coming to Canada to learn that the managers of 100,000 miles of railway, travelled over by 50 millions of people on this continent, had taken the first important step in the scheme of cosmopolitan time reckoning which, as an Association, it had officially and offensively refused to entertain."

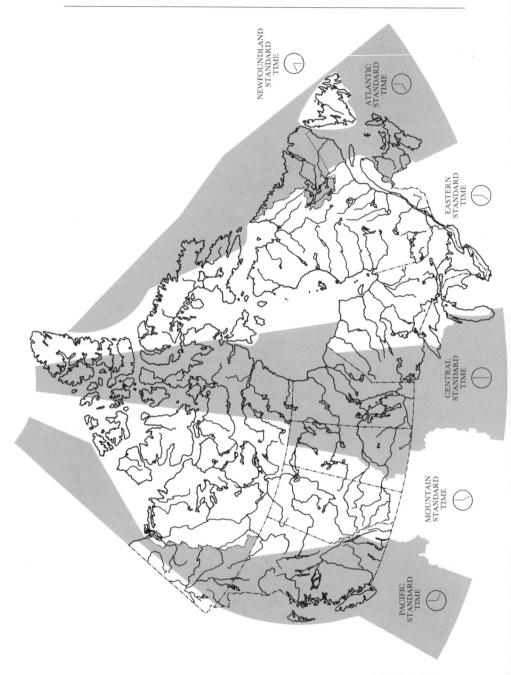

THE STANDARD TIME ZONES OF CANADA

When Fleming's idea for Terrestrial Time failed to gain support, he began instead to examine ways of averaging out the confusing differences in local times and coordinating them. He became a strong advocate of what has since come to be known as "Standard Time," and through the Governor General of Canada, his concerns were brought to the attention of British officials and governments around the world. In 1880, the Russian Imperial Academy of Sciences at St. Petersburg supported his proposals, and in that same year, Fleming approached the American Metrological Society and suggested establishing an international committee on Standard Time.

For the next five years, Fleming pressed home his ideas wherever he could find an audience. He attended international conferences in Venice and Washington and brought the matter before the American Association for the Advancement of Science as well as the American Society of Civil Engineers, who appointed Fleming chairman of a special committee on Standard Time. He wrote letters and circulated questionnaires to scientists and business people and to those who used time, along with calculations of longitude, to navigate on the open sea.

Regulating time also meant that a single meridian (line of longitude) had to be selected as the standard on which all calculations could be based. Several such meridians already served as the basis for various national systems of navigation, and in the discussion of time coordination, different countries had conflicting preferences. To avoid these national jealousies, Fleming originally proposed that a line should be drawn through the middle of the Pacific Ocean, while others recommended that it pass through Jerusalem or the great pyramid of Cheops. At the 1884 conference in Washington, however, Fleming's presentation finally settled the question by pointing out that the existing line through Greenwich, England, already served as the standard for two-thirds of the world's shipping industry, and in the interest of simplicity, it was eventually agreed that Greenwich should be adopted as the Prime Meridian, the foundation for the system of Standard Time.

Next to Fleming's notion of a single Terrestrial Time to be used by the whole planet, Standard Time is the simplest answer to the problems of regulating the world's clocks. Since the day is 24 hours long, the Standard Time system divides the globe along the north-south lines of longitude into 24 equal parts. The time in each of these is determined by setting the clocks to 12 noon as the sun passes directly over the line at the centre of the area, and in the same way that a local time was once

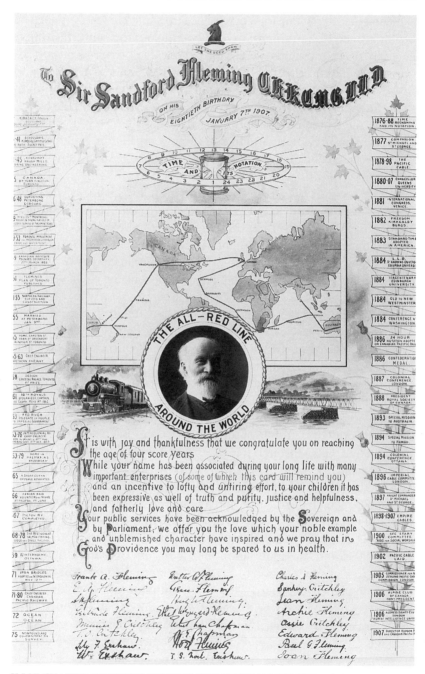

ILLUMINATED ADDRESS MARKING FLEMING'S 80th BIRTHDAY

calculated for different cities, a time is established for each of these regions. Each zone is one whole hour ahead of the zone to the west of it and one hour behind the zone to the east, and although clocks around the world show different times of the day, they all strike the hour at exactly the same moment. Travellers no longer experience unpredictable local differences, and when they do cross from one time zone to another, they need only change their watches by exactly one hour.

The fight for a standardized timekeeping system continued for several years before the 1884 International Conference at Washington established the fundamentals. Opposition took many forms, and alternative systems were put forward. Some people actually maintained that changes of any kind were unnecessary. Simon Newcomb, superintendent of the American nautical almanac, described the plans to regulate timekeeping as "too perfect for the present state of humanity."

By 1890, however, Fleming was able to report to the Royal Society of Canada that in addition to North America (which adopted Standard Time in 1883, a year before the Washington Conference), Great Britain, Sweden, Japan and the countries of central Europe had all moved onto the new system. And since the late 19th century, inhabitants of all but the remotest corners of the world have adopted Standard Time.

Sandford Fleming alone cannot receive full credit for the "invention" of Standard Time. The details of the new system were gradually hammered out over a period of years, and endless compromises were made. Some argue, in fact, that much credit should go to an American named Charles F. Dowd, who, in 1870, devised a scheme involving zones and standard time for use by the U.S. railways. As a railroad man, Fleming must have been familiar with Dowd's work, although the American's contribution is never formally acknowledged. Yet neither did Fleming himself ever claim credit for the creation of the timekeeping system that transformed the modern world.

A man possessed of a visionary imagination, Sir Sandford Fleming faced the world armed with a staunch reverence for the religious and political institutions of his day and a strong sense of his own worth. Unlike many men of his abilities, he was not a defiant individualist but, rather, a pragmatist who laboured for the common good. A dreamer of vast dreams that were both possible and practical, he entered fully into the business and pleasure of his beloved British Empire and there asserted his right to help shape the future of the world.

GEORGES-ÉDOUARD DESBARATS AND WILLIAM LEGGO

THE ILLUSTRATED NEWS

On April 6, 1868, a man named Pat Whelan placed a gun to the head of the Irish-Canadian politician Thomas D'Arcy McGee as McGee was about to enter his boardinghouse on Sparks Street in Ottawa. Then he pulled the trigger. Claiming to be drunk at the time, Whelan was actually a member of the Fenians, a group named for a legendary band of Irish warriors and dedicated to independence for Ireland. The Fenians were usually deadly serious in their intent. When Georges-Édouard Desbarats, the owner of the building where the shooting took place and a friend of McGee, mounted a commemorative plaque at the site of the murder, many said he would anger the Fenians. On January 20, 1869, his printing factory mysteriously burned to the ground. Desbarats' extravagant plans for the future of Canadian publishing disappeared under the collapsing roof beams and tumbling walls.

Yet the grandest flourishes of Desbarats' career began in the weeks and months following that fire. His intense energy grew directly out of a determination to rebuild, and within a year of the disaster, the first issue of his historic *Canadian Illustrated News* was released. The speed of his recovery was remarkable. As the years would show, however, overcoming impossible obstacles became something of a habit for Georges-Édouard Desbarats, who made a career of flirting with financial danger, bankruptcy and ruin. In the process, he played an essential role in the birth of modern illustrated journalism.

It is hard for a present-day reader to imagine the newspapers and magazines of the 19th century, with their close print and unrelieved columns of text. People have become accustomed to visual accounts of the news, and since the advent of television, those news pictures have shown the movement and excitement of events as they unfold. Magazines have inundated the world with bright, clear and often shocking images, and mass communication has lost some of its impact. In 1869, many readers had not seen a photograph of any kind, and newspapers and magazines contained mostly print with only an occasional hand-drawn illustration. A few publications in major cities such as London, Paris and New York regularly included illustrations, but these were a novelty. Generally, it was simply too difficult and costly to provide illustrations for the stories being reported.

Desbarats, however, insisted that illustrated journalism was not only desirable but also entirely possible. He dedicated his career to demonstrating that published illustrations were worth the trouble, and when he succeeded in placing a photograph on the cover of the first *Canadian*

THE DESBARATS BUILDING

Illustrated News in 1869, he turned the print medium in a completely new direction. Both the halftone technology that was used to reproduce the photograph and the *Illustrated News* itself were a few years ahead of their time. But they introduced a process that permanently changed not only the look but also the impact and function of magazines and daily newspapers.

A reader looking closely at the first *Canadian Illustrated News* would have seen that the cover photograph of H.R.H. Prince Arthur had been translated into countless tiny dots that had then been printed onto the front page of the new magazine. The picture was called a halftone — it captured all of the grey halftones between black and white — and had been produced using a halftone screen, a grid that divided the original photo into a series of tiny dots which could be reproduced by the printing plates and presses. Within a couple of decades, virtually every publication in the world would employ some sort of halftone technique, but Desbarats had acted first, displaying a confidence and foresight unmatched by even the publishers of the well-established illustrated magazines of New York and the capitals of Europe.

Desbarats' determination, in turn, nourished the genius of the magazine's engraver, a man named William Augustus Leggo. Although Des-

THE CANADIAN ILLUSTRATED NEWS, VOLUME 1, PAGE 1, OCTOBER 30, 1869

barats provided the financial resources and the editorial opportunity, it was Leggo who solved the practical riddles that others in his profession had been puzzling over since the invention of photography. He found an affordable and reliable means of printing numerous copies of a single original photograph. Together, the two men ushered in a new age of publishing.

Although his father and grandfather had both been successful printers before him, Georges-Édouard Desbarats almost became a lawyer. When his mother died in 1839, Georges was only a year old. His father remarried, and the young boy, sent to study with the Jesuits, grew up in a series of boarding schools. Perhaps as a result, he showed little interest in joining the family business. At the age of 21, however, he finished his studies in law and left for Europe, where he reportedly visited the small city of Pau, in France, thought to be the traditional family seat and home of the family printing business.

Upon his return to Canada, young Desbarats began to feel the weight and attraction of that tradition. Over the next six years, he became increasingly involved in printing, and during the years before the senior Desbarats' death in 1865, Georges and his father together published 13 book titles. By the time he had inherited the family fortune and responsibilities, he was clearly committed to the publishing industry and enthusiastic about its future.

Unlike his father, Georges Pascal Desbarats, who prospered as a manufacturer and merchant and held the position of Queen's Printer, Georges-Édouard seemed drawn to the more flamboyant possibilities of the literary and editorial work associated with the printing profession. His father had managed his businesses with a canny skill that won him considerable wealth, but though Georges, too, was a businessman, he was not a terribly practical one. Indeed, his business failures eventually outstripped his triumphs. Yet in his own way, Georges-Édouard Desbarats the dreamer was a great success. He proved better at envisioning and founding magazines and newspapers than at making them profitable; but over the course of his career, he injected a great deal of life into the Canadian publishing industry.

From 1859 to 1864, Desbarats worked with his father in the official capacity of Queen's Printer, the printer of all government laws and documents. For an additional five years, he shared the position with a man named Malcolm Cameron. During that time, he also published a number of books, foremost among them the complete works of Samuel de Champlain in 20 volumes — over 9,450 pages. The printing plates for this monumental work were burned with his Ottawa factory in 1869, but a copy had been sent to the editor, Father Charles Honoré Laverdière, in Quebec City, and Desbarats simply started all over again. The maps and illustrations required to do justice to the grand scope of Champlain's life brought Desbarats his first experience with the printing of illustrations, and from that point on, the notion of illustrated journalism never left him. The power of pictures not only gripped his imagination but seemed certain to win that of his readers. Never doubting that illustration would become an integral part of the print medium, he clearly foresaw the course of journalism in the late-19th and 20th centuries.

During his tenure as Queen's Printer, Desbarats had published an official magazine called the *Canadian Gazette*, but the *Illustrated News* was his first venture into commercial publishing. It was by no means his last. One year after the *Illustrated News* was successfully launched, he brought out a French companion magazine called *L'Opinion Publique*, another illustrated work with 12 pages, four fewer than the *Illustrated News*. *L'Opinion* merged a year later with *L'Étendard National* of Worcester, Massachusetts, and the new paper, with a total circulation of 13,000, was sold two years later. In 1871, Desbarats bought *The Hearthstone* and promptly restyled it as a handsomely illustrated quarto, a publication which was printed on large sheets with the text arranged so that each paper could then be folded into four pages with printing on both sides. Stories and serialized novels by both Canadian and American authors were featured, and along with its new look, the small literary paper was also renamed. Under the title *The Favourite*, it was sold across the continent from an agency office in Boston.

Along with his more literary efforts, Desbarats also produced what the modern publishing industry calls trade magazines. In 1873, he brought out *The Canadian Patent Office Record*, *Mechanic's Magazine* and *The Canada Medical and Surgical Journal*. He did contract printing for governments, one year publishing 13,000 copies per month of *Le Journal d'Agriculture* for the Quebec government. In 1878, he started an eight-page weekly humour magazine called *The Jester*, which featured "bright and spicy" editorial content along with good cartoons. There were numerous other projects as well. Throughout his career, Desbarats worked at a breakneck pace, accumulating and spending vast amounts of capital and eventually losing the fortune left him by his father.

In 1887, having been buffeted throughout his career by the vicissitudes of the publishing industry, he scored an enduring triumph with *The Dominion Illustrated News*, a magazine he founded with the financial support of several renowned Canadians, including Sir Sandford Fleming. Although Desbarats died in 1893, the *Dominion Illustrated*, thanks to the photographic reproduction technology that Desbarats had helped pioneer, survived him by many years. Ironically, however, Desbarats' financial failures — *The Canadian Illustrated News* and *The New York Daily Graphic* — because they represented ground-breaking efforts in halftone photographic reproduction, were the sources of his greatest satisfaction. They also earned him a place in history.

Desbarats' active interest in the technology of his day especially suited him to the task of making halftone photographic reproductions a reality. It is rare for a new technology to be put into use so soon after its creation, but Georges-Édouard Desbarats and William Leggo worked well together. As an engraver, Leggo was familiar with the demands of the printing trade, and Desbarats' curiosity kept him closely involved with advances in printing techniques. These two men succeeded with commercial halftone printing almost a full decade before anyone else managed to achieve the same goal.

Some may think it odd that Georges-Édouard Desbarats is mentioned at all in the story of the first halftone and the birth of photographic journalism. Desbarats, after all, simply bought the technology that put the first halftone photograph in his *Canadian Illustrated News*; he was the first customer for a process actually created by William Leggo. But if Leggo brought to the endeavour the inventive genius, Desbarats had the foresight to invest in a new technology and the courage to risk his fortune bringing it into regular use. For understanding the importance of Leggo's work and for translating it into a commercial reality, Desbarats takes a place beside Leggo in the history of invention.

But what of William Leggo? His story is difficult to trace; it is even further obscured by his relationship with Georges Desbarats. He might have left clearer tracks had he not sold the company that bore his name to Desbarats in return for financial support and the opportunity to use his talents and new techniques on a widely circulated illustrated magazine. With his three brothers, Leggo had been working as an engraver in Quebec as early as 1860, but in all likelihood, he grew up and was trained in Europe. He and Desbarats met in the early 1860s, and to facilitate their increasingly close partnership, Leggo moved from Quebec to Montreal in July 1869. Only four months later, their combined energies brought forth the world's first published halftone, and together, they planned even greater things. When Desbarats took over the firm of Leggo and Company in January of the following year, it was a financial arrangement that gave Leggo the freedom to continue experiments with new equipment and to refine the existing techniques.

Beyond these details, information about William Leggo is scarce. But we know of the revolution in photojournalism he sparked, and we have a photograph from the pages of *The Canadian Illustrated News* showing a robust and jaunty-looking man with thick side-whiskers leaning on the box of a large camera.

It is not surprising that so few clues to Leggo's life remain. The fraternity of printers and engravers was a secretive and suspicious one. An individual's technique for transferring printed images onto paper was the basis of his livelihood and not something to be lightly shared. Chemistry was not well understood, and the intricate procedures required to produce printing plates were not unlike the veiled recipes of alchemists and witches. Patent protection and the expanding commercial printing industry were changing all that, but those who experimented with the puzzles of printmaking and photography were a close-mouthed group nonetheless.

Just as Georges Desbarats had come from a long line of printers, William Leggo's heritage was that of an artisan. Leggo and his brothers were all second-generation lithographers. Their father had been among the first students of the master Johann Aloys Senefelder in Munich, Germany, at the printing house Senefelder established only a year after discovering the basic methods of lithography in 1798.

Senefelder's process actually had precedents in the 16th century and was quite uncomplicated in practice. He simply discovered a new way to use the fact that water and oil or wax or grease will not stick together. However straightforward his techniques, they nevertheless formed the basis for a great deal of the more complex printing technology that has followed, including Leggo's innovations. The lithography — literally "stone writing" — learned by Leggo's father consisted of first drawing a picture onto a block of smooth, flat limestone using a greasy ink. The stone was then wetted, and the water was absorbed by the stone everywhere except where the lines were drawn. A second application of greasy ink spread across the stone with a roller would stick only to the dry areas where no water had soaked in. When a sheet of paper was pressed into place, the original image was reproduced. In an alternative method, chemicals that could not pass through the ink of the original drawing would be used to etch around the drawing, eating away a layer wherever the surface was unprotected. The drawing then stood out as a series of raised ridges that could be re-inked and used to press

WILLIAM AUGUSTUS LEGGO, 1871

a copy of the drawing onto a page. This raised-impression technique eventually became properly known as letterpress printing.

Although others had been experimenting with similar etching techniques for centuries, Senefelder's process provided the first dependable and commercially viable means of replacing the painstakingly hand-carved wood blocks that were locked into the printing press along with the lines of type.

For Leggo's father and his father's contemporaries, lithography introduced a startling new technology. Printers immediately recognized that it presented possibilities for mass-producing clear line drawings and printing out illustrations. Only 27 years after Senefelder founded his printing house, a man named Joseph Nicéphore Niepce produced the world's first photograph, opening another realm of illustration. For the printers and engravers of Leggo's generation, combining the speed of lithography with the accuracy of photography became the ultimate quest. Printers everywhere raced toward the same goal: a means of printing photographs. Two generations after Senefelder's work in Munich, William Leggo was grappling with the mysteries of photography in Quebec City and inching his way toward a practical solution to the problem of mass-printing copies of photographs.

Photographs were originally produced by coating either metal or glass plates with light-sensitive substances and then focusing the light that reflected from a scene or image through a lens onto the plate. As it reacted to the light, the sensitive material would rearrange itself into a copy of the image being viewed. The accuracy of the results astounded people. It was not at all clear, however, how this kind of image could be transferred onto even one sheet of paper. Photographs had too many shades of grey to be easily reproduced using existing printing methods. A printing plate made from a photograph produced merely a smudge when it was inked up and pressed against a sheet of paper. Early photographs came about as a result of experiments by engravers looking for better ways to produce the printing plates used to transfer ink onto a page. Printers were using light instead of etching chemicals or tools to carve pictures onto the printing plates, and some of the earliest "photos" were simply failed attempts to produce those plates. When Niepce discovered that the images of nature itself could also be captured on similar plates with the same perspective and detail as viewed with the human eye, a new art was created. Since photography was virtually born in the printer's shop, it was almost inevitable that a printer would discover a means of copying photographs into the papers and books that were mass-produced in those shops.

Photoengraving in all its forms was the process of producing printing plates using substances that were sensitive to light. Attempts to print illustrations from photographic originals were a natural outgrowth of the continuing evolution of plate-printing techniques. Printers like Leggo were already working toward a practical means of producing printing plates that involved making rudimentary photographs of simple drawings on the metal plate. The plate would then be treated so that ink would stick only where the light-imprinted image was formed. In this way, an inked reproduction of the original picture could be transferred onto a sheet of paper.

Photographs, however, still presented a difficult challenge to printers. Although a lithographic plate could place black ink on a white page, even photolithographic techniques could not cope with the countless shades of grey that also make up a photographic image. Some additional stage was required, and in this, halftone screens played an essential role. Originally, a halftone screen was simply a piece of glass with two sets of fine parallel lines scratched closely together on the surface in a grid. A piece of fine gauze cloth was used in early experiments, and even the scratched-line method used by Leggo made the picture look as though it had been printed on canvas. Conceived by Fox Talbot, the English pioneer of photography, as a means of producing a positive print from the negative in the camera, the screen was placed in front of the image as it was rephotographed in the preparation of the printing plates. The halftone screen cut up the continuous shades of a picture into a composite of thousands of tiny dots, and in this way, black ink and a white page could be used to produce all the subtle shades of grey.

Without any dots at all, the blank page is white. But halftones work on the principle that as you move tiny black dots onto a piece of white paper, the paper appears to change colour. The eye sees ever darker shades of grey as the size of the dots increases, until finally, the page is filled in as solid black. In a printed photograph, the different shades in the picture are represented by areas where there are larger or smaller dots.

A good deal of experimentation was necessary to achieve an effective screen for creating halftones, and although American pioneers Frederic E. Ives and the Levy brothers, Louis and Max, standardized the manufacture of screens in the 1880s, it was one of the problems that Leggo had to overcome 20 years earlier. Halftone screens alone, however, did not allow for the mass production of photographs, and Leggo's true triumph was in discovering a practical means of photoengraving. He called it Leggotype, and with his engraving method, he could quickly and with relative ease copy any picture onto a printing plate and run off copies. Illustrations could be prepared for publications without hand-drawing them onto lithographic stones or carving them into printers' woodcuts. Illustrations could even be copied from other magazines and papers at a fraction of the cost of the originals; using a halftone screen, photographs from cameras could be transferred to a printing plate and onto the page. Compared with the painstaking and time-consuming task of creating a drawing or a woodcut, using photographs must at first have seemed like cheating.

As a skilled printer, Leggo had other techniques at his disposal, including engraving, lithographing, type printing and his own patented method of electrotyping — another specialized means of preparing printing plates. His unique specialty, however, remained the photolithographic Leggotype.

Desbarats and Leggo patented the process, then advertised it to win backing for their publishing plans. In May 1866, *The Philadelphia Photographer* reported:

"We have received from the inventors, Messrs. G.E. Desbarats and W.A. Leggo, of Quebec, C.E. [Canada East], some specimens of what they term 'Leggotypes,' or 'Photo-electrotypes' — done upon a common hand printing press — by their patented process. The object of the patentees is to produce electrotype plates of pictures, ready for common printing, like ordinary type printing, without engraving or other hand work. The process is briefly as follows: upon the varnished side of an ordinary negative, pour a solution of gelatine containing bichromate of potash. Dry, and expose the uncoated surface uppermost to light, which fixes that portion of the bichromate upon which the rays fall. Dissolve off the unfixed portion by dipping in warm water; drain, and we have a film upon the glass more or less raised, according to the strength of the lights in the picture. Take an impression of this film in plaster. Dip the impressed plaster in hot wax, and place the waxed surface upon a glass plate also covered with hot wax. The wax upon the plate unites with the wax upon the plaster, and the latter may then be removed, leaving upon the plate a facsimile in wax of the original photographic

DETAIL SHOWS ENLARGEMENT OF HALFTONE

gelatine film. The facsimile being now dusted with plumbago and electrotyped in the usual manner, a printing block in copper is produced, capable of use with printer's ink upon any press."

In simpler terms, Leggo's process involved coating a negative (just like the negatives for modern black-and-white photographs) with a substance that hardened when exposed to light. When a light was shone through the negative image, it was partially blocked out, but where it penetrated, it solidified those areas which were to show up dark in the final picture. So when the remaining unhardened "gelatine containing bichromate of potash" was washed away, a raised positive image was left behind like a rubber stamp, and the image was then transferred to the printer's plate. Ink was applied, and the image was pressed onto a blank sheet of paper to produce the final picture. Even a brief explanation suggests the complexity of printing techniques in the mid-19th century. Leggo's mastery of new techniques earned him the financial backing he needed to implement them; in turn, his mastery supported Georges-Édouard Desbarats' faith in illustrated journalism. His inventive skills played a crucial role in the fundamental shift toward the assumption, unique to the 20th century, that the exchange of information and telling of news should be accompanied by a visual image.

The Canadian Illustrated News survived for 14 years, genteelly presenting book reviews, gossip and Victorian novels in serial form. Short on social comment, it did not grapple with contentious political issues. Yet most 19th-century periodicals were fiercely partisan and were used to spread the personal opinions of the people who owned them. The Canadian Illustrated News distinguished itself by the even-handed and objective style it brought to the issues it reported. For historians in the century since it was published, it has also proved to be a valuable repository of photographs that were unavailable from any other source.

On December 28, 1883, the Illustrated News folded, according to the then publishers, "for the simple reason that its issue is not remunerative to the Company who publish it." Desbarats himself had sold the magazine in 1874 when its circulation stood at 7,000, and he withdrew entirely from the endeavour in 1879 after a 10-year involvement, a decade in which he had also busied himself with many other projects. For a number of years, the magazine's unique format kept it afloat in a very competitive and unpredictable industry, despite the fact that Canada's small population made the survival of a national publication unlikely. The true measure of Leggo and Desbarats' accomplishment, however, was their launching of The New York Daily Graphic in 1873, the first illustrated daily in the world. Huge amounts of capital were attracted to this project, and the confidence of the important investors rested on Desbarats and Leggo's demonstrated success printing both hand-drawn and photographic illustrations.

The remarkable achievements of The Canadian Illustrated News have often been overlooked by historians of photography. Credit for the first published halftone is often given to a man named Stephen H. Horgan, who printed the first newspaper photograph in The New York Daily Graphic in 1880. The revolution that actually began in 1869 with the first issue of The Canadian Illustrated News is often mistakenly ascribed to the famous American paper. In any case, there has been no historical injustice. The men who brought about the advances made at the Illustrated News were the very people who went on to establish the New York paper. Horgan's historic photograph was printed with a method he learned from William Leggo, using one of Leggo's half-

Canadian Illustrated News

PROSPECTUS.

[T]he imagination is so closely linked to the perceptive [fac]ulties, that the speediest and surest way of reaching [the] mind and impressing thereon facts and objects, is to [place] them vividly before the eye (that main feeder of the [ima]gination,) either in their reality, or in the drama, or even through their image painted or engraved. Hence the popularity of illustrated books and newspapers, through the latter of which especially, millions receive knowledge of the resources and features of various countries, and of occurrences therein, of which they would otherwise remain utterly ignorant. In the neighbouring States, and in Europe, illustrated papers flourish by scores, but Canada has no such medium of communication with its own people or the outside world. No counterpart have we to the *Illustrated London News*, *Le Monde Illustré*, *Harper's Weekly*, &c. And yet, how much have we not [in] this vast Dominion, our noble home,—how much of [ma]jestic nature, of grand architecture, of historical monu[]ments, of floating palaces, of thriving manufactur[es], worthy of illustration in the highest style of the Engrave[r's] art? How many interesting events, important ceremoni[es], elegant gatherings, now pass away forgotten, which, [re]produced by the artist's skill, would in later years [be] recalled with pleasure and prove instructive and amusi[ng] to generations yet unborn? A Canadian illustrated pap[er]

[A] weekly Journal of current events, Literature, Science and [Ar]t, Agriculture and Mechanics, Fashion and Amusement, [P]ublished every SATURDAY, at Montreal, Canada, by GEO. E. [DE]SBARATS.

Subscription, in advance, ... $4 per annum.

Single Numbers, ... 10 cts.

... will be entitled to Six Copies for one year.

City subscribers served by Carriers. Postage to distant places *Prepaid by Publisher*. Remittances by Post Office Order or Registered Letter, at the risk of the publisher.

Advertisements received to a limited number, at 15 cents per line, payable in advance.

LEGGO & CO.,

Leggotypers, Electrotypers, Stereotypers, Engravers, Chromo and Photo-Lithographers, Photographers,

AND

GENERAL PRINTERS BY STEAM POWER,

Office: No. 10, Place d'Armes, MONTREAL. Works: 319, St. Antoine St.

PROSPECTUS, 1870, WITH PROMOTION FOR LEGGO AND COMPANY

tone screens. Unfortunately, the New York venture eventually resulted in Desbarats' bankruptcy, and he was forced to withdraw from the publication. But if the significance of Leggo and Desbarats' careers as pioneers of photojournalism is recognized, it is clear that *The New York Daily Graphic* represented their greatest contribution to the development of the print medium.

The idea for the *Daily Graphic* arose after Desbarats and Leggo had already launched the *Illustrated News* and were looking for new ways to exploit the advantage that, for the moment, they held over virtually every other printing operation in the world. The speed with which Leggotype photoengraving could prepare an illustration must have suggested the idea, and they realized, no doubt, that by printing a daily paper with illustrations — not necessarily photographs — they would earn the distinction of doing something that had hitherto been entirely impossible. No one had ever been able to prepare illustrations quickly enough to keep pace with the daily reporting of the news, and the inevitable public excitement over what they would be doing guaranteed success. All they needed was a large enough market, and they settled on New York City as the place to attempt the scheme.

The road to the new newspaper began with advertisements in *The Canadian Illustrated News*, a call for investors who would underwrite the effort. By describing the proposed publication — eight pages, four of which would have pictures — and their plans to illustrate the day's events "while public excitement, enthusiasm or indignation were still at their height," Desbarats and Leggo hoped the advertisement and many others like it would create confidence in both themselves and the Leggo patents. The proof of their success came on March 4, 1873, when the first issue of *The New York Daily Graphic* went on sale.

There were many skeptics. Experts before them would have claimed that no one could observe an event on one day and have an illustration prepared and transferred onto the appropriate printing plates by the next day. And yet that is what the two Montreal businessmen planned. When they succeeded, they demonstrated for the first time that illustrated news was both possible and desirable.

Leggo remained associated with the paper for several years, but Desbarats' connection probably ended as early as 1874, when, beset with financial woes, he was forced to declare bankruptcy. Since the fire in his plant five years earlier, he had been in a precarious position, and his troubles were aggravated by the management extravagances of the

New York office, which carried on business in a grand style (including sponsoring a failed attempt to fly a balloon across the Atlantic Ocean). Desbarats ended up having to sell off most of his holdings.

Neither Desbarats nor Leggo became rich from the New York effort. Nor is either man particularly well remembered by history. But Leggo was able to continue to perfect a working technology which allowed printing of a kind that had never been done before, and Desbarats fashioned the technology into a commercial reality — a paper that thousands of people held in their hands daily. If imitation is the truest form of flattery, however, their profession has honoured them every day of this century. Every illustrated magazine and newspaper in the world owes something to the two Canadians who first put a photograph on the cover of *The Canadian Illustrated News* and declared that the daily news should be illustrated too.

MABEL BELL AND THE AERIAL EXPERIMENT ASSOCIATION

KITES, WINGS AND FLIGHT

Only a gentle breeze drifted over the excited spectators gathered on the frozen bay in late February 1909, but up above, a single propeller drew a giant pair of handmade wings through the winter air. Like a kite rising on its own rushing wind, the first aircraft in the British Empire soared and fluttered through the Cape Breton sky. In a subsequent letter to her daughter, an onlooker described the "glorious sweep" of the craft turning out over the bay. She recounted its rough landing — necessary to avoid crashing into trees on the headland — after spending six breathtaking minutes aloft, and she enthused about how the pilot, Douglas McCurdy, a young member of the Aerial Experiment Association (AEA), had passed closely by her. Mabel Gardiner Bell had not had a clear view the day before, when the *Silver Dart* made the first manned flight in Canadian history, and now, the sight of the craft as it freed itself from the earth and slipped through the sky was a personal triumph.

Mabel Bell's husband Alexander became famous when he created the telephone in 1876. The revolutionary device had brought the couple a vast fortune by the time its inventor was only 35. It had also made Bell a celebrity in an age that looked upon inventors as its greatest heroes; it placed him in the company of queens, kings, emperors and great scientists. Yet the invention of the telephone overshadows his other interests and accomplishments, and the world forgets that during Alexander Bell's long life, he was a pioneer in other areas as well, one of the most important of which was aviation.

Those who are aware of his work in aviation may not realize that Bell was only one member of a group of enthusiasts known as the Aerial Experiment Association. Founded in 1907, it included Frederick "Casey" Baldwin, a young engineer from Ontario who became Bell's partner in many of his later ventures; Thomas Selfridge, a U.S. army officer convinced that aviation held future possibilities for the military; J.A. Douglas McCurdy, the son of Alexander Bell's friend and secretary, Arthur McCurdy; Glenn Curtiss, an American designer of internal-combustion engines and the world record holder for the fastest mile — a feat he accomplished on a motorcycle he had built himself; and, the founder and sponsor of the association, Mabel Bell. While Alexander Bell's colossal reputation tended to dwarf the activities of his colleagues, his theories were not, in fact, among the most fruitful that emerged from this unique group. Each member possessed different

THE SECOND CANADIAN FLIGHT OF THE *SILVER DART*, FEBRUARY 24, 1909

skills, and all had their own ideas about aviation. Separately, they might have accomplished little; united, they succeeded gloriously.

Much credit is owed to the person who fell most completely in Alexander Bell's shadow. Had Mabel Bell been a man, the formation of the Aerial Experiment Association and its subsequent achievements would have been attributed largely to her. It was Mabel Bell who suggested that the small group of hobbyists take their task more seriously. It was she who, through regular evening discussions with her husband and by correspondence when they were apart, made considerable contributions to its progress, and it was she who provided the financial backing that made possible the group's transition from imaginative speculation to practical experimentation. The sale of a piece of land in Washington, D.C., left to her by her father, had earned her $20,000, and she donated the whole of this sizable sum to the aviation association. As a result of her dedication and financial support, the AEA began its work in earnest. Because of her intervention, it earned an important place in the history of air travel. Inventors dream of fantastical machines, and successful inventors make them a reality. For the AEA, Mabel Bell was a catalyst in that transformation.

The Bells' home at Baddeck, Nova Scotia, was a remote and unlikely place for advanced aeronautical research. Named Beinn Bhreagh — Gaelic for "beautiful mountain" — the country estate was not even

SHEEP AT BEINN BHREAGH, THE BELLS' HORTICULTURAL EXPERIMENTS

accessible by a good road. After a long steamer ride across the Bras d'Or Lakes just to reach the town, visitors were ferried across the bay to the Bells' wharves on the opposite shore. The Bells had originally purchased land at Baddeck in 1886 for a summer residence. Alexander could not stand the heat of Washington, where they had lived since the early 1880s, and had even gone so far as to drain the swimming pool in the basement of their house and set up an office there, into which he pumped ice-cooled air. With visions of a peaceful retreat, the couple bought a small cottage near town. They named it Crescent Grove, but the locals dubbed it "the house on stilts" after the Bells had it jacked up to add a new first floor. In the years that followed, however, they bought up the parcels of land that formed the large headland opposite the town; there, they eventually built their well-known mansion on the hill, with its round towers and sleeping porch and its spectacular view of the bay below.

Beinn Bhreagh did not remain a quiet retreat for long. The Bells seemed to bring with them all the excitement of an ever-changing world wherever they went. Completed in 1893, the main house was soon the centre of a web of paths and roads that connected the various outbuildings and stretched from the wharves at the shore all the way to the neat rows of sheep houses on the hill, where Alexander and Mabel conducted horticultural experiments.

At times, an almost carnival air of excitement, of strange and playful progress, pervaded Beinn Bhreagh. And guests were always welcome. Family and visitors came and went, sometimes on holidays, sometimes on business and often to witness or join in the research Alexander Bell had been conducting with kites. For years, the inhabitants of Baddeck looked on — occasionally in disgust, more frequently with bemused tolerance — as Bell and his often distinguished visitors stood out on the windy hills flying a bewildering assortment of kites: huge double saucers and box kites, kites shaped like four giant wheels joined by steel frames up to 15 feet long. Bell was convinced that an engine on a kite could perform the same task that a child does when running and pulling a kite on a string. As he worked through the problems of constructing larger and larger kites, Bell became even more certain that the contraptions he flew from the hilltops — sometimes so large they had to be pulled behind a horse — would eventually show him the means for human flight.

One of the most important and fortunate guests to visit the Bells' east-coast residence was a young man named Casey Baldwin, a graduate of engineering from the University of Toronto. For years, Mabel Bell had watched her husband at work and, in frustration, had eventually concluded that he needed a well-trained and practical-minded partner for his various endeavours. After the unimaginable success of the telephone, Alexander Bell possessed more than anyone needed of earthly rewards. His satisfaction lay simply in showing the world that new and useful things were possible, yet he too rarely brought his projects to a conclusion. In a letter to young Douglas McCurdy, who was attending school in Toronto, Mabel Bell suggested he bring home with him anyone he thought might be interested in Bell's work — someone with the training in the practicalities of design that Alexander lacked, someone who could take up the work that the distinguished inventor was likely to neglect. Accordingly, McCurdy approached Casey Baldwin, who accepted without hesitation.

The grandson of the Honourable Robert Baldwin, one of the Fathers of Confederation, young Baldwin was not only an able student of engineering but also a famous athlete of the day in his hometown of Toronto. His visit to Beinn Bhreagh signalled the beginning of perhaps the happiest and closest working relationship of Alexander Bell's life, a partnership that extended well beyond the two men's shared interest in aviation. Even their first meeting seemed auspicious, for Baldwin arrived in Baddeck shortly after Alexander Bell had made one of his most intriguing discoveries.

There is an old party trick that involves using six toothpicks or matchsticks. The challenge is to produce four identical triangles using only the pieces provided. The task for the person laying out the sticks on a tabletop seems impossible, for the sticks cannot be broken and they cannot overlap. The solution is to lay the first triangle flat and stand the remaining three pieces on end inside it, leaning them together like a tiny tepee. The shape thus formed is called a tetrahedron, and as Alexander Bell discovered during his work with kites, this three-dimensional figure possesses great structural strength. For Bell, it represented the answer to one of his most pressing problems.

Human flight was impossible, claimed many scientists of the day, because a surface much larger than a simple kite could accommodate would be required to achieve enough lift for an object to leave the ground. That, they reasoned, created an insurmountable problem, since as the surface area of a structure increases, the weight of that structure also increases, and it does so at a much greater rate. Elementary geometry seemed to prove them right. Even Alexander Bell's scientist friend Simon Newcomb concluded that flight could never be achieved. A small kite might be able to pull against a string with 10 pounds of pressure, but a kite 20 times as large would not be able to pull in the same wind with 200 pounds of pressure. The kite would simply be too heavy to get off the ground.

The strong yet lightweight pyramids seemed to solve the problem. Two kites pull twice as hard as one, so Bell reasoned that a number of small cells, like a flock of kites, would provide a large kite with abundant lifting power. Each little cell would act as an individual kite, and joined side by side, each tetrahedron could share common members with the ones adjacent to it. Thus the weight of the kite would be reduced dramatically. A kite made up of many of the small pyramids would have plenty of surface area. The tetrahedral structures would provide strength and rigidity without the need for heavy bracing, and the kite would remain light enough to lift into the air. These conclusions formed the basis of experiments Alexander Bell had begun when Casey Baldwin joined the family at Baddeck.

The discovery that lightweight materials could be made into an incredibly strong pyramidal frame was a radical advancement in en-

THE BELLS WITH A MOTORIZED KITE, A TETRAHEDRAL STRUCTURE

gineering, and Alexander Bell did not fail to see its implications. He worked out ways that tetrahedral building components could be mass-produced, and he envisioned the endless uses to which they could be put. A notebook even shows his crude, childlike drawing of a train with a scribble of smoke rising up from the engine as it makes its way across a trestle constructed of the triangular forms. Enthusiastic about the possibilities, Mabel Bell first consulted with an independent engineering firm and, thus reassured, insisted that the value of tetrahedrons be demonstrated by building an actual structure. Baldwin's first challenge was to assist with the erection of an 80-foot-high observation deck on the windswept hill above the Bras d'Or Lakes. "Mr. Baldwin begins tomorrow on the construction of a steel tetrahedral tower," Mabel wrote in a letter to her daughter. "He expects to get the whole thing up with just a jackscrew instead of the expensive and complicated machinery usually necessary, so perfectly are the cells fitted one into another."

The tower itself was a great success, and the pair worked out systems of standardized production for the component parts and patented each of these techniques. Yet the rest of the world did not catch on to the benefits of such lightweight structural design for several years. Long before then, Baldwin and Bell had turned their attention to aeronautics. One year later, Douglas McCurdy finished his studies and returned to Baddeck to join in their experiments.

MABEL BELL. THE PULL OF A KITE

Over the years, the Bell family had remained consistently dedicated to the idea of spreading scientific knowledge as widely as possible. Loyal patrons of the scientific world, they were well known for their generous support of and contribution to a variety of projects, among them *National Geographic*—of which Mabel Bell's father had been a founder—and a magazine called *Science*. Their lively and open capacity for engaging like minds had made them something of a rarity in the often competitive world of invention. It was no surprise, then, that U.S. army lieutenant and West Point graduate Thomas Selfridge had got wind of the experiments taking place in far-off Baddeck. Having met Selfridge in Washington, Alexander Bell himself arranged with President Theodore Roosevelt to have the young officer assigned as an observer. Once in Cape Breton, Selfridge, too, became caught up in the excitement. As the determined group grew, it flew great kites from the hills and towed them behind horses or behind boats on the bay, dreaming of the day when humans might fly.

From the beginning, of course, the Bells knew well that whatever machine might be constructed would require an engine—not just any engine but a very efficient, lightweight engine. With this challenge in mind, Alexander Bell approached Glenn Curtiss of Hammondsport, New York, who also became a regular guest in Nova Scotia.

With the arrival of the young men at Baddeck, Bell's experiments took on a new, more serious air. Selfridge brought meteorological equipment with him, and suddenly, accurate wind-velocity recordings replaced Alexander Bell's picturesque estimates based on nothing more scientific than how rough the waves appeared on the bay. The pulling power of the kites was recorded with spring scales rather than merely noting the size of the rope that had snapped when a kite broke away. In some respects, however, the whole enterprise still looked somewhat like a group of boys with miraculous dreams and extravagant toys. In the summer of 1907, Mabel Bell changed all that.

Since their marriage, the Bells' considerable financial dealings had been left in Mabel's capable hands. At their wedding ceremony, the young Alexander Graham Bell had turned over to his wife all but 10 of his shares in the newly formed Bell Telephone Company. Years later, their daughter pointed out that his unusual and grandly romantic gesture had, in truth, very nicely rid her father of all responsibility for the mundane intricacies of the family bookkeeping. Despite the fact that women of the day were assumed to have no head for business, Mabel Bell quietly took on the task for which her proper young lady's education had done nothing to prepare her. In the decades that followed, she proved a skilled manager of the vast fortune that flowed from the telephone patents, and she was therefore no stranger to the value and uses of money when she laid her proposal before Alexander Bell and his enthusiastic young visitors.

Mabel Bell understood that theories of flight must be tested against real winds; she knew, too, that the work at Baddeck had foundered and that further experiments would cost money. Rather than borrow or dip into the family coffers, she chose to sell a piece of her own property to provide backing for a proper research effort. In effect, Mabel threw down the gauntlet, challenging the group of men to make a proper job of their research. By so doing, she effectively hired the first of history's many aeronautical-research teams.

And so, in October 1907, the Aerial Experiment Association was born. It was solemnly decided that they would undertake research for a period of at least one year. Each of the younger men agreed to a salary, with the exception of Selfridge, who continued to draw his army pay. Alexander Bell contributed his laboratory facilities, and together, the group trooped off to Halifax, where Alexander Bell added a touch of excitement to the proceedings by convincing the American Consul-General to add his signature to the official document they had drawn up. By contract, they agreed to pursue not just Alexander Bell's ideas but the various plans of each, with the "common aim 'to get into the air' by the construction of a practical aerodrome driven by its own motive power and carrying a man . . . ."

The work of the new association began with Alexander Bell's huge tetrahedral kite, called the *Cygnet*. Consisting of over 3,400 pyramidal cells, each covered in hand-sewn bright red silk, it looked like a giant slab of scarlet honeycomb, and calculations and tests had indicated that it should be able to lift the weight of a person. Although the *Cygnet* had no engine, its prototype design enabled it to be towed into the air like a normal flat kite, and the local steamship company agreed to lend the association a vessel, called the *Blue Hill*, which was capable of pulling the great weight. Accordingly, in December 1907, the AEA loaded the *Cygnet* onto a specially built barge and headed out onto the bay. Selfridge crawled into the passenger space and was covered with rugs for warmth, and when the *Blue Hill* gathered speed, the *Cygnet* lifted gently into the air and rose to the remarkable height of 168 feet. For several minutes, it flew steadily at the end of its rope. Even Bell, who dreamed of a craft so secure that it could be tethered to the ground and held aloft on a breeze while the pilot climbed down to the earth on a ladder, could not have desired a more stable craft. As it descended, however, a cloud of smoke belched from the steamer's stack and hid the kite from view. The man stationed on the steamer with an axe ready to cut the tow-rope did not see the kite as it touched down into the water. Although Selfridge managed to slip clear, the *Blue Hill* drove on, dragging the kite behind it until it was in pieces. With a resounding splash, the AEA ended its first season at Beinn Bhreagh with both a success and a disappointing setback; although their aircraft had lifted a passenger high into the sky, they faced the prospect of starting all over again. It was to become a familiar pattern.

The AEA, of course, was not the only group interested in flight. Despite the fact that the Wright brothers' success in 1903 at Kitty Hawk, North Carolina, was regarded by some as merely an unsubstantiated rumour, many people still lived and breathed the idea of human flight. Since a lightweight engine was essential for any flying machine, Glenn Curtiss's factory at Hammondsport attracted many aviation enthusiasts. And it was to Hammondsport that the young members of the AEA migrated in the winter of 1907-08, while the Bells went on to Washington to attend to their affairs. In Hammondsport, they met inventors with plans for all manner of extravagant flying machines — helicopters and aeroplanes and ornithopter contraptions with flapping wings. Having destroyed the *Cygnet,* the AEA quickly set about constructing its first aeroplane.

The word "plane" simply means "surface," and an "aeroplane" rises into the sky due to the action of air moving across the broad surfaces of its wings. The stability of the multicelled *Cygnet* had convinced Alexander Bell that large, flat wings were not the safest means of flight, but the AEA had promised from the beginning to pursue the ideas of each of its members. Now the others designed a machine based on the glider principles of a man named Octave Chanute. Like the craft used by the Wright brothers, who also owed their start to Chanute, theirs would be a biplane — two immense wings bound together with a system of struts and wires. Although they worked as a team, the AEA's members nonetheless agreed that each of their crafts would be named for one of them and would provide that member with an opportunity to work out the ideas he considered most important. Drome No.1 was therefore designated *Selfridge's Red Wing,* a reference to the heavy red silk, left over from the kite experiments, that was used to cover its wings. Actually, Casey Baldwin provided most of the craft's innovations, but he modestly credited Chanute and claimed that any other ideas were a result of the fact that he did the drawings for the group. The other members eventually insisted that he have at least one patent in his own name in recognition of his contributions.

As it turned out, Baldwin also had the honour of giving the *Red Wing* its first test. By March 1908, construction was complete, and the *Red Wing* stood ready. Forty-three feet across, the two sets of wings curved so that they dipped closer together at the tips than at the centre. Flexibility in sections of the wings was designed to provide stability, and the world's first enclosed cockpit was constructed both to protect the pilot and to make the craft more streamlined. On March 12, the air was calm and the conditions clear, and with Selfridge away, Baldwin was elected as pilot. Supported on sleigh runners, the *Red Wing* was run out onto the ice of Lake Keuka, New York, where the wide frozen expanse left plenty of room for building up speed. Curtiss fired the engine, and Baldwin scooted away, racing at 20 miles per hour over the ice. About 150 feet down the lake, he eased back on the control lever. Miraculously, the *Red Wing* lifted into the silent air and rose to an altitude of 10 feet. Flight! After several long moments of suspense, Baldwin thumped back onto the ice, turned the machine around and hopped merrily into the air once more, only to be waved down when his companions, chasing wildly down the lake on skates, noticed that a strut had broken.

By measuring the gap in the runner tracks, the group discovered that the first public flight in North America had covered 318 feet, 11 inches. After a moment of excitement while Baldwin groped wildly under his seat to switch off the engine, the *Red Wing* settled to a stop without mishap. Five days later, however, during its second flight, the fragile craft smashed down onto the ice, and the AEA returned to the workshop to begin construction of their second machine.

Drome No. 2, *Baldwin's White Wing,* incorporated an innovation that became an essential component of every airplane ever built. Even the short flights of the *Red Wing* had demonstrated the need for a mechanism that would control the plane's tilt from side to side. Baldwin had managed to fly the *Red Wing* by throwing his weight left and right as the wings tipped under him. But on the second machine, he introduced wing flaps — ailerons — that became the means of steering any aircraft. The AEA thought to make the mechanism automatic by attaching the flaps to a harness worn by the pilot. As the wings tipped, the pilot would naturally lean in the opposite direction and thereby pull the flap just the right amount; the system worked beautifully, just as flaps of one kind or another have continued to work ever since. The *White Wing* also employed a tricycle undercarriage and, again, was the first air machine in North America to adopt this innovation. Baldwin and Selfridge both made short flights, and when Curtiss's turn came, he soared for a distance of over 1,000 feet. Only days later, however, McCurdy was walking with crutches and their second plane lay in ruins.

Each crash, each apparent failure, taught the members of the AEA valuable lessons. Their third machine, Curtiss's Drome No. 3, contained all of the features they had produced so far. In addition, Curtiss had managed to improve the engine, and the *June Bug,* as it was nicknamed, had a brief and glorious career. After disappointing tests, Selfridge realized that air must leak through any porous cloth, and he suggested soaking the wing fabric with an oil. This "doping" dramatically improved the machine's lift, and it became standard practice for as long as wings were constructed of cloth on a lightweight frame. The *June Bug* flew so well that the AEA decided to attempt a standing challenge made by *Scientific American,* and on July 4, 1908, Curtiss, in the *June Bug*, became the first person to fly a heavier-than-air machine for a measured distance of one kilometre under test conditions. In later years, he would also win the distinction of being the first human to successfully take off from and land on water.

It seems appropriate that J.A.D.McCurdy, as the most skilled aviator in the group, should have lent his name to the AEA's most successful craft. *McCurdy's Silver Dart,* again named for its colour, was covered with a nonporous rubber-coated material and embodied all of the

THE *SILVER DART* ON THE ICE OF BADDECK BAY, FEBRUARY 24, 1909

group's rapidly expanding knowledge about flying machines. It, too, proved a remarkable success.

The intense camaraderie and spirit of cooperation enjoyed by the AEA's members had been incredibly fruitful. They had put five crafts aloft, four of them successful, self-powered, heavier-than-air machines, and they had done so in less than the one year they had allowed themselves. Yet even as Mabel and Alexander Bell considered ways to extend the period of the AEA's contract, an almost inevitable tragedy tore a great hole in the closely woven fabric of the association. Thomas Selfridge was reassigned to the U.S. army's newly formed Aeronautical Board, and the Wright brothers, prodded by the AEA's winning of the *Scientific American* trophy, finally made their work public in the United States and began conducting tests for the military. When Orville Wright crashed during a flight on September 17, 1908, his passenger, Thomas Selfridge, died of the injuries he sustained. Throwing a sad cloud over the AEA's other distinctions, Selfridge's death was powered aviation's first casualty in North America, and two weeks after what Mabel Bell described as "this breaking of our beautiful association," the AEA's one-year contract came to an end. "It had been a band of comrades on a grand adventure," Mabel wrote, and it would never again be the same.

Nevertheless, with the *Silver Dart* still in Hammondsport and such rapid progress being made, the Bells decided to extend the life of the AEA for another six months. Mabel advanced another $15,000, and the *Silver Dart* was moved to Beinn Bhreagh for additional tests on the frozen surface of Baddeck Bay. There, in the late winter of 1909, the first flight in Canada took place. Although the others pressed for another trial that same day, Alexander Bell — by now having grown wary and perhaps with an eye on the history books — insisted the *Silver Dart* be put safely away so that no further incident could mar the occasion. In the days that followed, repeated flights demonstrated both the qualities of the machine and the increasing skill of the pilots. McCurdy made several flights, including one that lasted a full nine minutes. Those sparkling winter days on Baddeck Bay marked the apex of the Aerial Experiment Association.

As the six-month extension drew to a close, the Bells, Baldwin and McCurdy discussed making the AEA a joint-stock company with the purpose of manufacturing aerodromes for sale. To their consternation, they learned that Glenn Curtiss had, in fact, already taken a partner and established the Herring-Curtiss Company. In the years that followed, the Bells supported Baldwin and McCurdy in the formation of the Canadian Aerodrome Company, and although it attracted a great deal of attention, the venture failed to win the government support it needed. Governor General Earl Grey visited Baddeck in order to see the young men who could fly; Mabel Bell observed in a letter that on that day, even the seals, attracted by all the movement and noise, climbed out on the ice to watch the excitement. Tests at the army base at Petawawa, however, failed to impress the military, and after producing only two more planes, the company folded.

With the help of his young friends, Alexander Bell built two more tetrahedral-celled "dromes": the *Cygnet II* and the *Oionos* (named for the bird of Greek mythology). With a more powerful engine, the *Oionos* might have succeeded, but it managed to lift its undercarriage off the ground for a distance of only one foot.

Alexander Bell's concern with safety had convinced him that planes should take off from and land on water. The attempt to develop technology for this purpose eventually led to research on hydroplanes — literally, "water wings" — which lift a boat up into the air and support it on a small surface, allowing it to slip quickly over the water. Baldwin and Bell experimented with the idea of a craft that would first rise onto the hydrofoils and then lift into the air and fly. As the war loomed

HER HUSBAND LOOKS ON AS MABEL BELL PILOTS THE *HD-4*, 1919

in Europe, they attempted to use the same technology to produce a high-speed submarine chaser. For 12 years, their vessel, *HD-4,* held the world water-speed record at 70.86 miles per hour. A photograph of the time shows Bell standing on a wharf gazing intently into the distance where Mabel Bell, by then a grandmother, pilots the thundering craft, with its twin aircraft engines, over the waters of the bay.

The historical significance of the Aerial Experiment Association remains difficult to assess. Although it made substantial contributions and earned a number of historic distinctions, its serious work was not undertaken until several years after the rumours of the Wright brothers' successes at Kitty Hawk had begun to circulate. The glory of being first, however, had never been its aim. Nor was financial reward its motivation. Alexander Bell, in fact, had warned his young partners that even if they succeeded, there was no assurance of profit. He knew from experience that costly patent litigation followed any invention — his own telephone patents had been challenged in the courts more than 600 times. But the primary inspiration for the group had been that its members simply wanted to prove that flight was possible and to advance the infant science of aeronautics. Nothing compared with the sheer excitement and satisfaction of that search. The Aerial Experiment Association wanted to play a part in the revolution that was about to burst upon a skeptical world.

With the disbanding of the AEA, Glenn Curtiss's company began to produce aircraft that were among the very best of the early machines.

THE BELLS CELEBRATING THE SUCCESS OF THE TWIN-ENGINED *HD-4*

Curtiss relied heavily on AEA discoveries that had been signed over to him by the other members in return for cash and shares in his company. The patents for these innovations eventually passed into the hands of the U.S. government, which, on the eve of World War I, cleared away confusion in the young aircraft industry by purchasing all patents, including those of the Wright brothers and Curtiss. Thus the dramatic successes of the AEA were swallowed up by the explosion of activity which followed the first demonstrations that flight was possible. In a few short years, a public that had openly scoffed at the pioneers of flight now clamoured for more, encouraged through public lectures by people like Alexander Bell, who worked tirelessly to promote aeronautics and its innovators.

The members of the AEA went on to other endeavours and new achievements — Curtiss to his new aircraft company, the Bells and Baldwin to experiments with hydrodromes and Douglas McCurdy to further adventures as an aviator (and, years later, to a term as Lieutenant Governor of Nova Scotia). March 31, 1909, marked a sad day for the group as its members gathered in the hall of Beinn Bhreagh. Mabel Bell was not present for the meeting, but the association that had begun in her thoughts ended with thoughts of her. As association secretary, McCurdy read a special resolution into the minutes:

"Whereas the members of the Aeronautical Experimental Association individually and collectively feel that Mrs. Alexander Graham Bell has, by her great personal support and inspiring ideas, contributed very materially to any success that the Association may have attained, Resolved that we place on record our highest appreciation of her loving and sympathetic devotion without which the work of the Association would have come to naught.

"It is reluctantly moved by Mr. Baldwin and regretfully seconded by the Secretary that we dissolve."

With those words, the AEA quietly disappeared. The members took away with them their memories of workshops and engines and wings in pieces and the soaring thrill of flight. In return, they left behind a long list of practical innovations and a special gift to the world — the certain knowledge that human flight, the dream of centuries, was finally a reality.

THOMAS WILLSON

CANADA'S INDUSTRIAL REVOLUTIONARY

North of the St. Lawrence River, the Saguenay and its tributaries tumble down the weathered face of the Canadian Shield. Torrents of water dropping from the cliffs plunge into gorges cut deep by the centuries. In the late 1800s, limitless forests lined the waterways, and people began to whisper about the untold fortune in timber standing on the banks of rivers wide and strong enough to carry that wealth to distant mills and shipyards. Anyone who went looking for permission to exploit this natural resource, however, found that Thomas Leopold Willson had already been there.

An inventor and industrial developer, Willson had spent years gathering timber and water rights up and down the Saguenay River Valley. At one time, he controlled more acreage than any other person or company in the province, and he had big plans. His intention was not merely to take trees from the land, for when he looked out over the Quebec wilderness, he recognized something far more valuable than wood. He saw raw, unbridled energy tumbling along the river valleys. He saw enough hydroelectric power to drive the wheels of an immense industrial development. In fact, like the prophets of the Old Testament, Thomas Willson saw into the future.

Thomas Willson did not live to see the industrial development of the Saguenay River, but his vision tells us something vital about this profoundly practical Canadian. Driven by the rare combination of a rich imagination and common sense, Willson was never afraid to take an informed risk to realize his dreams. In pursuit of funding for yet another venture, Willson was eventually forced to mortgage his Quebec interests to the American tobacco tycoon James Buchanan Duke. Duke, in turn, sold the land to industrialist Arthur Vining Davis, who established the vast aluminum industry that made the area world-famous. Indeed, the town of Arvida, Quebec, one of the region's major centres, takes its name from the first two letters of each of Davis's names. Although no equivalent honour commemorates Willson's original contribution, the omission would not have caused him any concern; he had always preferred making things happen to gaining public renown.

Willson's early years were not easy. Born on a farm near the village of Princeton, Ontario, on March 14, 1860, Thomas Leopold Willson was the grandson of the Honourable John Willson, a member of the Legislative Assembly of Upper Canada and the man known as the "Father of the Common Schools Act," in recognition of his role in establishing public education in the province. Thomas's father, a minister with an entrepreneurial bent, lost the family home and farm when he used it to guarantee a loan for a friend. A move to Bridgeport, Connecticut, followed, but it had no happier an ending. Willson's father died when his oldest son was only 14 years old, after an unsuccessful attempt at becoming a manufacturer.

Although he had enjoyed the early benefits of an ambitious and industrious family life, Willson was nonetheless left in difficult circumstances by the death of his father. Inventors, however, are unusual people who somehow manage to preclude predictability by finding unorthodox solutions to their problems. Young Willson clearly inherited this trait from his mother. A proper widowed woman in the late 19th century might understandably have thrown herself on the mercy of her relations, but Rachel Sabina (Bigelow) Willson insisted on supporting her young children herself. After her husband's death, she moved the family to Hamilton, Ontario, where she scandalized the neighbours by taking in boarders and teaching painting and Spanish guitar. There, high school sharpened Willson's natural talent for physics and chemistry, but it was from his mother that he learned equally valuable lessons about independence and determination.

Whatever Willson did, he did boldly, and that was true even in the first years of his career. At the age of 19, while other boys sought positions as office clerks or as apprentices with carpenters, barrel coopers or wheelwrights, young "Leo" Willson had already identified more unconventional ambitions. His fascination with chemistry had been encouraged by his teachers and tolerated by his mother. But the evil-smelling experiments he conducted in his makeshift basement laboratory at home took their toll. The local blacksmith, John Rogers, agreed to let an empty loft above the smithy in return for helping out around the forge. Willson established a rough laboratory in his loft, and before long, his employer had become an eager assistant, working with Willson first on the construction of a steam-driven generator and then on a system of experimental arc lights. When not quite 21, Willson acquired a patent for these lights — the first of 60 different patents he would be granted during his lifetime — and launched his tumultuous career.

Few people can imagine the incredible excitement of the early years of electricity. In the 20th century, this raw magical power has been tamed and made to flow quietly through wires buried in the streets of our cities and in the walls of our homes. For pioneers like Willson, however, it must have seemed as if their handmade generators unleashed fierce genies — powerful, unpredictable forces and sparks that burned the gases of the air and were capable of melting solid objects. The entire history of electricity is a story of controlling that power, of making it safe and reliable, and it is not surprising that young Willson encountered difficulty when he attempted to transform his electrical arc lights into a successful commercial enterprise.

The first electric light in Hamilton, Ontario, shining from Willson's laboratory window above the Rogers forge, attracted such attention that it had to be moved to Dundurn Park where spectators could gather to look. Willson became the talk of the town and soon had orders from local businessmen for lighting in factories and in the Royal Hotel. But his inexperience and the uncontrolled power of his own electric system now betrayed him. His newly patented dynamo could not produce a steady supply of power, and the lights developed a disturbing habit of blinking on and off without warning. Furthermore, if even one light was turned off, a surge of power would rush through the system, blowing out all of the other lights as well. Contracts were cancelled, and Willson, who was compelled to repay all the money he had received in advance, soon found himself in trouble. The young inventor and local hero slipped badly into debt, and in 1881, he had no recourse but to leave town. It was not to be the last time that Willson's creative ambitions and the world of commerce clashed.

From Hamilton, Willson travelled to New York City, the proud centre of technological development in 19th-century North America. The faint-hearted support for his inventions at home had been discouraging, but in the bustle of New York, he set to work immediately. He changed jobs frequently over the next few years, working originally for the Fuller Electric Company and later for the Remington Gun Company. He also took on research assignments for a group interested in using electric furnaces to smelt ore and for a railway company that wanted to replace the oil lamps in its trains with a system of arc lights. But his first successes in Hamilton had taught him that he worked best when he was in charge of plans and assignments, and in 1886, he established a company to develop a new patented lighting system.

No noteworthy success came out of these early ventures, but Willson sharpened his research skills and learned by trial and error about the often hard realities of the business world. His first company folded due to the inefficiency of his partners, and over the next few years, he

ORE FURNACE, BASEMENT OF WILLSON'S OTTAWA HOME

set about learning how to manage money and how to produce and market his products. He acquired a shrewd business sense to go along with his powerful creative imagination, and when a combination of hard work and luck brought him the discovery that would change his life, he was ready to take advantage of his good fortune.

In 1891, Willson met Major James Turner Morehead, a prosperous mill owner from North Carolina. Morehead had no experience with either chemistry or the use of electric furnaces but was certainly familiar enough with the idea of generating power for his mills to understand the plans of the confident young inventor. For some time, Willson had been working with the idea of producing aluminum, still a relatively new metal and fabulously expensive. He felt that the existing technique for producing the strong, lightweight material from sodium was much too complicated and far more costly than it needed to be, and he believed that by using calcium, a much simpler process could be found. All he required was startup money and a steady source of electricity for a furnace. The possibilities were obvious to Morehead, and along with another man named George Seward, he agreed to finance the Willson Aluminium Company.

From the beginning, there was something magical about the little generating plant and laboratory on the bank of the small river running through Morehead's land in Spray, North Carolina. Willson and the assistants he hired were like a team of ancient alchemists seeking ways to produce gold from base metals. They planned to place inexpensive materials into a furnace and then extract valuable aluminum. In his notebooks, Willson even speculated that they might stumble onto a way to produce diamonds. Yet as they searched for shiny metals and glittering gems, all they uncovered was frustration. Unbeknown to Willson, better methods for producing aluminum had already been discovered in both the United States and France.

The Willson Aluminium Company might have been a waste of time had its founder not decided to look for ways to offset the costs of his fruitless experiments. He began working with other materials such as copper and succeeded in producing a very expensive batch of metallic bronze. That was not the solution to his problems, however, and he decided to search for a means to produce metallic calcium. Again he failed, but this time, his failure proved very interesting indeed.

In the late 19th century, electrochemistry was still not an exact science. Researchers mixed materials together and exposed them to great heat, but they could not always foresee what kind of reaction would take place. Many times, they would open their furnace only to find an unrecognizable melted blob inside, and that is precisely what happened on May 2, 1892. Willson instructed his assistants to combine specific amounts of coal, lime and tar and heat them to 5,500 degrees C. The hot mixture was then removed from the furnace and dropped into a pail of water to cool. When the material hit the surface, the day's routine experiment suddenly erupted into boiling excitement. The bucket began to churn and bubble. A gas was obviously escaping from whatever had been thrown into the bucket, and when things were calm once more, the water was no longer clear but white.

The metallic calcium that they thought they were producing combines with water to form hydrogen, so the presence of a gas was not too surprising. But Willson recognized that the violent nature of the reaction was unusual. He wondered if the gas would burn or perhaps even explode, and he decided to conduct a simple experiment. Like a scientific comedy team, he and his assistants prepared a test. On the end of an old fishing pole, they fixed a piece of oily rag. Then, as Major Morehead's son John held it, they lit their impromptu torch, and everyone stood back. Another chunk of the mysterious grey substance from the furnace was tossed into the water, which again started to boil like a witch's brew. Young John advanced across the room. As he brandished the burning rag over the pot, a flame leaped between it and the bubbling water. When he pulled the pole back, the flame disappeared, only to reappear as soon as the torch was brought near once more. Ribbons of soot leaped writhing into the air and settled about the room, but Willson and his team hardly noticed; after months of failure, they had finally made a discovery. They did not know exactly what they had found, but a gas that burns is always an intriguing and potentially useful commodity.

In the months that followed, Willson set about trying to identify both the grey mixture from the furnace and the gas produced when the mixture was added to water. Recognizing that his own talents were of a practical nature and that he would need the assistance of more theoretical minds, he enlisted the help of staff at the nearby University of North Carolina. A few months later, he sent off a sample to William Thomson, the noted Scottish scientist at the University of Glasgow. It was the same year that Thomson would be made Lord Kelvin in recognition of his far-reaching work in engineering and physics. Thomson wrote back and advised Willson that the material was calcium carbide. The bubbles rising up out of the bucket of water were identified as acetylene gas.

In truth, "Carbide" Willson, as he was thenceforth known, did not invent or discover anything new in that small laboratory in Spray, North Carolina. His genius, however, was revealed in the work he did during the months that followed. Calcium carbide and acetylene had both been seen in laboratories before, but nobody had found a use for them. The fortunate accident that took place in Willson's furnace gave him a means of producing the grey material that was a millionth the price of any other method. Willson conducted experiments that mixed water into the calcium carbide to produce gas. He determined how to freeze the acetylene back into a solid and soon discovered that the best use for the gas was to burn it for the bright, white light it produced. A laboratory curiosity became an important new product.

When kerosene became available in the 1850s, it virtually led society out of the dark ages. So much brighter was it than any of the alternatives that people found its light startling. Now, decades later, tests had revealed that acetylene burned with a flame more than 12 times as bright as that of kerosene. Ironically, the man who began his career looking for ways to replace burning lamps with electric lights had found the ultimate fuel — a gas that would delay the triumph of electricity for many years to come.

FIRST CALCIUM CARBIDE PLANT IN CANADA, BUILT BY WILLSON, 1896

Bright, white sunshine is made up of different colours of light. Of these, the human eye can distinguish red, blue and yellow because various objects reflect the colours hidden in that light. Even modern household light bulbs do not produce nearly as pleasant a glow as sunshine but are actually quite yellow, like photographs taken indoors at night. Willson's acetylene, however, burned like the sun, its light containing every colour of the spectrum. Botanists were able to grow plants in dark rooms using only acetylene lamps. Soon, everyone had ideas and suggestions, and there was nothing that the new light could not do. Eventually, it was used in everything from miners' hats to automobile headlights. It was a process that would bewitch anyone: Water mixed with a grey powder becomes sunshine!

The flurry following Willson's discovery resembled that of a gold rush. New uses were found every day for the acetylene, and though many of the companies that sprang up to take advantage of the new markets failed, the industry itself survived and flourished. In the midst of the initial excitement, Willson and Morehead negotiated the sale of the patented carbide process to the newly formed Union Carbide Company. In 1895, Willson married Mary Parks, and a year later, he moved back to Canada a wealthy man. In the years that followed, Union Carbide went on to become a gargantuan multinational corporation, but its inception had been a direct consequence of Willson's work. Like the prospector searching for gold who finds instead an immense copper deposit, Willson had reason to be well pleased with his so-called aluminium company.

Willson's profits from the sale of his patents gave him the means to build factories and a company of his own, and over the next few years, he laboured to establish carbide works in Canada, where he still held the rights to his discovery. Beginning in Merritton, Ontario, he situated his developments where an abundant supply of hydroelectric power could feed the sizable furnaces needed to produce calcium carbide on a commercial scale. His Merritton works included the first hydroelectric plant in Canada and the largest constructed in North America to that time. Watching the failed attempts of several American companies had no doubt taught Willson a valuable lesson about the importance of locating factories where raw power and raw materials were easily accessible.

The years following his return to Canada brought Willson great success and a wealth that seemed to grow of its own accord. A resourceful entrepreneur, he made canny business arrangements, including a financial partnership with the Right Honourable James Sutherland, a businessman from Woodstock, Ontario, where Willson had built a lavish mansion to house his family, and a cabinet minister in Wilfred Laurier's Liberal government in Ottawa. It was Sutherland who convinced Willson that he must move to the capital city and find his place in the country's circle of power and influence.

By 1904, Willson had established two more factories: on Victoria Island, on the Ottawa River; and in Shawinigan, Quebec. Even then, he could not keep up with the demand for his products and had to license others to go into business in competition with his own companies. He supervised experiments with street-lighting systems and attempts to freeze acetylene to facilitate shipping. And just when electricity threatened to steal the lighting business, it was discovered that oxygen and acetylene could be burned together with a flame so hot, it could cut solid steel. The Brooklyn Navy Yard in New York used the torches to cut portholes in armour plate as early as 1907, and the same oxyacetylene torches that have been used ever since became popular, revolutionizing the industrial world. Willson's business doubled once more.

Willson remained quietly restless. He belonged to a handful of influential social clubs in Ottawa and mixed with the leaders of the land, people who came regularly to visit him and his wife at their Metcalfe Street mansion. William Cornelius Van Horne, the man who took over from Sandford Fleming as chief engineer of the Canadian Pacific's transcontinental railroad project, became a partner in several of Willson's companies. Willson's fortune continued to expand and multiply, and yet he was merely supervising the explosive growth of an industry he had brought into existence. The interesting work was completed, and he itched for something new. He had already set about amassing water and timber rights along the Saguenay River when an incident involving one of his inventions temporarily claimed his attention.

One of the most exciting uses of Willson's magical gas was as a bright beacon on the waterways. Navigation buoys using acetylene gave off a brilliant glow, and the conversion to the new gas was quick and enthusiastic. Like a symbol for the whole acetylene industry, the new buoys were a modern marvel that made shipping safer and easier. Like any flammable substance confined within a closed container, though, acetylene is highly explosive, and the buoys with their lanterns rigged up over large storage tanks were potential bombs waiting to go off. In April 1904, the inevitable happened. One of those bombs, a beacon at the dock in Kingston, Ontario, finally detonated while it was being refilled. Two more buoys were set off by the blast, which demolished the refuelling vessel drawn alongside; the boat's captain and three of the crew were killed. Suddenly, the bright symbol of progress looked more like a lethal menace.

Willson's reaction to the news was swift and characteristic. Perhaps he already had the solution in mind; perhaps the crisis unleashed the inventive energy that his business responsibilities had suppressed for several years. In any case, only a few months later, he filed for patents on a new type of navigational marker. The problem with the old design had been that pressurized tanks on the buoys had to be filled from another pressurized tank on a boat, which in turn often had to be filled at the factory. Each of these steps was potentially dangerous. Willson designed the new buoys so that each one produced its own supply of gas automatically as it sat rocking gently in the shipping channel. Instead of acetylene, each buoy contained a supply of calcium carbide. Water mixed with the dry powder at a slow, steady rate, and a reaction just like the one in the original experiment in his Spray, North Carolina, laboratory produced the gas necessary to light the beacon. The new markers were just as bright but entirely safe. They were also remarkably durable.

THE SAFE ACETYLENE NAVIGATIONAL BUOY

INTERNATIONAL MARINE SIGNAL COMPANY, 1906-1909

Willson, of course, could not simply design a solution to the problem and stand idly by while others developed it. He immediately set up manufacturing facilities, and by 1906, his International Marine Signal Company was in full swing. With orders from over 40 countries, the venture not only salvaged the reputation of acetylene as a manageable illuminant but was also a huge success in its own right. Located on Ottawa's Wellington Street, the signal company guaranteed Willson yet another fortune.

Willson's schemes raced through his mind like a field of runners, with one taking the lead and then another. Plans for the Saguenay River project were under way; plants controlled by his companies turned out tons of calcium carbide and acetylene every day; the factory on Wellington Street had begun gearing up as orders for navigational aids poured in from around the world; and in the midst of all the excitement, the inventor withdrew to the laboratory constructed in the basement of the Willson family home on Metcalfe Street. As early as 1895, a pair of scientists named Caro and Frank had demonstrated that calcium carbide could also be used to "fix," or capture, nitrogen and thereby make it possible to store it as a solid. Willson the chemist realized that meant his existing factories — which made calcium carbide and acetylene — could also be used to produce a powerful nitrogenous fertilizer. He wanted to explore the possibilities.

It was one of the most exciting projects of Willson's career. Fertilizer

BASEMENT LABORATORY, WILLSON'S METCALFE STREET HOME, OTTAWA

was already in use around the world, but most of it came from the guano fields of Chile, where bird droppings were scraped from the rocks and shipped around the tip of South America. With that supply almost exhausted, agriculture faced a crisis of global proportions, and Willson was one of the scientists prepared to confront the problem. The modern world takes fertilizers for granted, but at the turn of the century, artificial fertilizers must have appeared to be magical powders. Sprinkled on a field, they caused stronger, greener and larger plants to appear than had ever grown there before. Willson became interested in the so-called superphosphate fertilizers and withdrew to his private laboratory where, in short order and with apparent ease, he perfected the most powerful fertilizer anyone had ever seen. Then, as always, he took out the necessary patents.

During this period, Willson moved his family to a summer estate at Meech Lake. Set in the beautiful Gatineau Hills north of Ottawa, the property was a paradise of scenery and restful quiet. (To keep in touch with the bustle of business in the city, however, Willson had a telephone installed and invented and patented what came to be known as the party-line system.) The mansion was surrounded by landscaped grounds and orchards and looked out over the peaceful water of the mountain lake. It perfectly suited the quiet tastes of Mary Willson, who had never felt entirely at home amid the whirlwind of activities at their house in the capital.

That same mountain water also pleased her husband. To Willson, still water represented potential hydroelectric energy, and a lake — especially a lake in the hills — had to have an outlet of some kind where the water could be directed into the gates of a generating station. No longer intrigued by his various well-established business enterprises and frustrated by their demands on his time, Willson began to sell off his holdings. In 1909, a Buffalo firm bought the International Marine Signal Company. Two years later, Willson sold out his carbide factories and patents worldwide. And although disappointed in further attempts to assemble financing for the Saguenay River project, he pushed ahead with the fertilizer scheme on his own. In 1911, he dammed the small river below Meech Lake and built a private hydroelectric station hidden in the woods and a factory for the production of the superphosphate agricultural products.

In an attempt to win financial backing for his new schemes, Willson continued to sell off his companies and mortgage his properties. Then, he met James Duke, and in 1913, he chartered a private train to guide the American industrialist into the Saguenay wilderness. The extravagant travel arrangements paid off when Duke agreed to forward Willson $1.5 million, but it was a fateful deal for the inventor. Duke accepted the Saguenay property as security for the loan, and when Willson could not meet the repayment requirements, he lost control of the very timber and water rights that he needed to proceed with his plan. The Saguenay was the foundation of his schemes, and without it, the huge financial house of cards he was constructing came apart. He had wagered several fortunes on the endeavour, and suddenly, it seemed he had lost.

The setback might have crushed almost any other person, but Willson was merely slowed down. To Willson, money was the servant and by-product of good ideas. He did not see how personal financial woes made his plans any less valuable, and apparently, others agreed. Although Willson had sold the worldwide rights to his carbide processes, the strange political and legal realities of the day meant it was still possible for him to establish a carbide works in Newfoundland — the east-coast colony was not yet a member of the Canadian confederation. By July 1914, he had guarantees for over $10 million in support from financiers in England. During the time it took for legislative approval of the developments, however, the outbreak of World War I cut off all export capital from Britain. Never an isolationist when it came to finan-

WILLSON'S MEECH LAKE HYDROELECTRIC STATION, 1912

cial backing, Willson set out to make alternative arrangements. But at the age of 55, while searching for new funding sources, he suffered a heart attack and died alone in his New York hotel room.

For decades, the world neglected the remarkable story of Thomas Willson and his inspiring accomplishments. Unfounded rumours circulated; magazine articles written in the 1950s even suggested that Willson had become despondent over financial setbacks and had wandered away from home to end his life in a lonely hotel room.

In fact, Willson's last years surged with all of the intensity and energy that had characterized his entire life. Plans for the development of the Saguenay River Valley had been superseded by experiments on superphosphate fertilizers, which in turn became part of a breathtaking vision for the industrial development of Labrador and Newfoundland built around hydroelectric generation, carbide works and pulp and paper. His life was cut short as he raced full speed toward a future that the world would not realize for another 50 years. The untimely death of a great inventor and an insatiable student of science and technology probably delayed the industrial development of Newfoundland by half a century.

THOMAS LEOPOLD WILLSON, AGE 54

Carbide Willson's career ended abruptly, but his influence persisted. A quiet man with an almost intuitive understanding of the potential of electricity and chemicals, Willson conceived plans on an immense scale and undoubtedly had a profound effect on the patterns of Canadian industrial development in the 20th century. But even he did not foresee the significance of his greatest accomplishment. Henry Ford's introduction of assembly-line manufacture is often identified as the second great wave of industrial expansion, but it was acetylene, with its ability to cut steel into any shape, that moved industry out of the age of the blacksmith and into the modern era. As a businessman and even more as an innovator, Willson would have been pleased both that his navigational buoys were replaced by something better and that brighter, cheaper, more convenient electric lights won out over acetylene lamps. He loved change and improvement, and it is impossible to guess what further contributions he might have made had he lived on into the years of spectacular technological progress between the two European wars. Had he survived, he would have seen acetylene shaped into a host of new products, from industrial solvents to synthetic rubber and plastics. The self-taught inventor who had begun his career with a single quavering light shining from the window of a Hamilton smithy would no doubt have approved.

REGINALD FESSENDEN

ON THE AIR

In the last years of the 19th century, electricity lit up the night with a cleaner, brighter light than had ever been seen before. It powered streetcars and began to drive the wheels of industry at greater and greater speeds. Unfortunately, hot wires, poorly insulated and plastered into the walls of people's homes, acquired a deserved reputation for starting fires that threatened to kill the young electricity industry. At his laboratories, Thomas Edison responded to the menace by handing the problem over to an untrained, inexperienced 21-year-old Canadian named Reginald Aubrey Fessenden, who found an answer and, in the process, rewrote humankind's fundamental understanding of the structure of atoms, the building blocks of the material world.

The son of a poor Anglican minister, Reginald Aubrey Fessenden came by his intellectual powers naturally. His mother was the journalist and well-known nationalist Clementina Fessenden, and her father was Edward Trenholme, inventor of the grain elevator, the grain cooler and the railroad snowplough. The Trenholmes were a family of strong-willed, independent-minded people, and the house that Clementina and her siblings kept in Montreal while they attended school was a meeting place for young people drawn to the Trenholmes' modern ways and outspoken opinions. One of those young people was Elisha Fessenden, and on January 4, 1865, he and Clementina were married. In the fall of the following year, their son Reginald was born.

Reginald's earliest remarkable skill was language. The boy who had read Edward Gibbon's *The History of the Decline and Fall of the Roman Empire* at age 7 was teaching Greek and French at Bishop's College School in Lennoxville, Quebec, by the time he was 16. Along the way, he had won a scholarship to De Veaux Military College in Niagara Falls, New York, and attended Trinity College School in Port Hope, Ontario. At Bishop's, Fessenden taught classes during the day and went to classes in the evenings to "gain some insight into higher mathematics," as he put it in a letter home.

Fessenden made it a lifelong habit to gain insights and to confront difficult problems by returning to first principles and grounding himself in the most essential and fundamental knowledge he could acquire. Although he left Bishop's to accept a teaching position at the Whitney Institute in Bermuda, those first studies in mathematics marked the beginning of his extraordinary career. An uncle, Cortez Fessenden, also played a crucial role in his early development. An educator and co-author of the first Canadian physics textbook as well as an amateur inventor, Cortez taught his nephew an abiding respect for pure science and mathematics while also imbuing him with a deep enthusiasm for the glories of technological progress. Throughout his career, Fessenden would approach each new problem by rejecting accepted theories and rebuilding from the ground up.

Compared with the frenetic activity of the following years, Fessenden's stay in Bermuda was a quiet time, a time for self-examination and for gathering strength. On his first day there, he met Helen Trott, a fellow teacher whose family had settled on the island. Working together and later sharing the island's limited social life — which was often centred around the Trott family dinner table — the two young people became friends as well as intellectual allies. Helen must have glimpsed something trustworthy in the eccentric and intense young man. They became engaged, even as Fessenden made plans to leave the island. A remarkable woman herself, Helen had likely drawn her own conclusions about Reginald Fessenden and his schemes. Yet even she must have experienced some doubt when Fessenden announced that he would go to New York and acquire the learning and experience he needed to become — as he had already predicted he would — the inventor of wireless telephones. Dissatisfied with teaching and charged with equal measures of scientific enthusiasm and self-confidence, Fessenden sailed from Bermuda to New York City in 1886. After taking a room in a boardinghouse, he presented himself at Thomas Edison's Llewellyn Park laboratory

Fessenden was not the first to make that particular pilgrimage. Many ambitious young scientists had flocked to the inventor whose creations were changing the face of society and whose fame had already made him a legendary hero of American culture. In response to the calling card sent in by Fessenden, Edison fired back a note asking a single question: "Do you know anything about electricity?" With uncharacteristic modesty, Fessenden, who already possessed an impressive grasp of mathematics as well as a self-taught understanding of the theories behind electricity, answered, "No, but I learn quickly." Edison terminated the correspondence by declaring, "I already have enough men who know nothing about electricity." A full year passed before Fessenden found himself back at the Edison laboratories.

During those first months in New York, Fessenden took on writing assignments for the *New York Herald Tribune*, turning out articles that earned him $5 apiece. To gain the practical experience with electricity that he lacked, he passed his time at construction sites pestering the foremen until he finally landed a job testing the wires that Edison's own company installed in the streets of Manhattan. He proved so adept at handling the machinery and taking careful readings with the "galvanometer" that, within months, a series of promotions placed him back where he wanted to be, at Edison's side doing laboratory research and helping to shape the ideas of the future into practical reality.

The quality of Fessenden's mind and the freshness that his self-education brought to existing problems impressed Edison immensely. He encouraged the young man's propensity for avoiding the pitfalls and prejudices of accepted theories, and together, they worked on constructing improved dynamos. Reminded of their first exchange of notes, Edison conceded regretfully that he must indeed have been in a foul mood that day. Already he knew that Fessenden's ignorance could be more valuable than the lifelong experience of other men.

When Edison faced the critical need for flameproof wire insulation, he charged Fessenden with the task of finding a material that could not only resist oil, water and acids but could also be folded and twisted like rubber without cracking during installation. It would be decades before plastics provided a solution to the problem facing Fessenden, and although there were many materials at that time which resisted corrosion, very few offered the necessary elasticity.

The assignment was deceptively simple. Instead of experimenting with various compounds, Fessenden set about tracking down the root of the problem, eventually conducting studies of even the most basic structures of matter. As Edison had undoubtedly expected he would, Fessenden immersed himself in the theories of physics and chemistry and, ignoring the conventional wisdom of his day, tried to find out for himself why certain materials were elastic and why they caught fire when heated. Eventually, he concluded that excess hydrogen atoms made rubberlike substances flammable and that hydrogen could be replaced by chlorine atoms without making the resulting material too brittle. Subsequent experiments proved him right. The pungent chlorine soaked his skin, hair and clothes and imparted a strangely unromantic scent to the letters he wrote to his fiancée in Bermuda; but in the end, he delivered the necessary insulating compound, thereby guiding the electricity industry past a major roadblock.

Fessenden's research into the nature of matter led him to two conclusions: that the components of atoms possessed matching positive and negative charges which held them together; and that the quality of elasticity in rubber was determined by the nature of those electrical relations. Such insights brought him into direct conflict with perhaps the most famous and respected scientist of his day, Lord Kelvin, the great University of Glasgow physicist. "Obviously," argued Lord Kelvin, "the fact that rubber particles stick together cannot possibly be due to electricity. Every physicist knows that it is because of gravitation." A few years later, Fessenden claimed that "an inventor must never be intimidated by what appear to be facts when he

REGINALD AUBREY FESSENDEN

knows they are not." His laboratory work contradicted Kelvin's position, and his published articles subsequently proved the point. Twenty years later, physicists following the lead of giants like Niels Bohr and Ernest Rutherford would begin to talk about atoms in terms similar to those used by 25-year-old Reginald Fessenden, who discerned the basic structure of the atom on the way to creating a better fireproof rubber insulation for electrical wires.

Part of Thomas Edison's ambition as a young man was to use the fortune he had earned from his early telegraph inventions to establish a facility that would provide "inventions-for-hire" as well as pursue new projects. Not long after Fessenden's first success, Mr. Pratt of the Pratt & Lambert Paint Company Ltd. paid a visit to the Edison laboratories. Mr. Pratt was looking for ways to improve the quality of his varnishes. Edison sent him to see young Fessenden, by now the head of the chemistry division. Fessenden had experimented with hundreds of substances in his work on insulation and almost immediately suggested mixing Zanzibar gums into varnish, an innovation that produced a beautiful shiny finish that was both cheaper and longer-lasting.

Pratt and Lambert were so impressed that they offered the self-taught chemist a full partnership in their company with an extravagant annual salary, doing their best to lure Fessenden away from the Edison fold. Fessenden, however, had other plans. The seeds of many of his greatest inventions had already been planted. Edison's facilities, with their powerful emphasis on transforming raw science into technology, suited him perfectly. In the extensive library and laboratories, Fessenden was educating himself, preparing to pursue his greatest dreams. He turned Pratt and Lambert down, just as he would refuse other tempting offers in the future. In the often-impoverished years that followed, he never gave any sign that he regretted his decision.

Fessenden's three-year tenure with Edison undeniably made him a chemist, but his success with wire insulation was followed by experiments with electricity as well. He tailored the special dynamo that Edison required for his moving-picture equipment and ransacked the vast Edison technical library for information about wireless voice transmission, combing through dozens of journals and contemporary reports. In 1887, when Germany's Heinrich Hertz, the discoverer of electromagnetic radiation, succeeded in causing a spark on one side of his laboratory to ring a bell on the other side of the room, he also caused a great leap of excitement in Reginald Fessenden on the other side of the ocean. With his co-worker Arthur Kennelly — the man who would one day discover and explain the nature of the earth's ionosphere — Fessenden waited impatiently for the first written reports about "Hertzian Waves." In time, Hertzian theory occupied his every waking hour.

In the late 1880s, the Edison companies suffered a series of setbacks, and Fessenden and his colleagues found themselves unemployed. Refusing to let this interfere with his plans, he married Helen Trott in September 1890 in New York City. Years later, one of Helen Fessenden's favourite stories was of Reginald sitting beside her in Central Park after the wedding ceremony confessing that he had spent all of his money on a 22-karat-gold wedding ring and a diamond brooch from Tiffany's. He had not considered the problems of food and a room, and the couple had to use Helen's money to purchase their train tickets to Chippewa, Ontario, where they spent their brief honeymoon visiting with the Fessenden family.

Fessenden's work now began in earnest. His time with Edison had exposed him to the leading edge of both science and practical innovation and had transformed a talented young dreamer into a strictly disciplined researcher and inventor. He found a position in Newark, New Jersey, with the United States Company, a subsidiary of the famous company founded by George Westinghouse, inventor of the air brake for trains. After being laid off once again in 1892, he accepted an academic post at Purdue University, in Lafayette, Indiana.

During his brief time with Westinghouse, however, Fessenden had made yet another discovery that profoundly affected the young electricity industry. In the 20th century, the light bulb has become synonymous with brilliant ideas. It had indeed been the perfect invention, a stroke of Thomas Edison's genius. But Edison held the patent on the light bulb, giving him exclusive control of a market that George Westinghouse wanted to pursue. Only a few years after the light bulb's discovery, Reginald Fessenden was handed the task of reinventing the little gadget. And that was exactly what he proceeded to do.

The original light bulb relied on fragile platinum wires to pass electricity through the glass of the bulb. The material was expensive and the technique was patented, so lighting remained costly and limited in its uses. But in short order, Fessenden circumvented the existing patents and made a significant improvement in design. In place of platinum, he discovered an iron alloy and a nickel alloy that could be fused to the glass of the bulb and used to supply electricity to the filament inside the vacuum of the bulb itself. The design won new patents and earned Westinghouse the contract for the 1893 exposition at Chicago. Tens of thousands of people saw the miraculous new lights, and a vast popular market was born. The cheaper, longer-lasting bulbs revolutionized the industry.

During the same period, Fessenden came up with the solution to a problem plaguing the designers of electric motors and transformers: electric motors were overheating, and there appeared to be no remedy. With his unique understanding of the nature of atoms, Fessenden concluded that the cause of excess heat was the behaviour of carbon atoms in the steel used to build the motors. This in itself was a considerable discovery. He then set about designing a new kind of steel, determining that carbon atoms in the steel could be replaced with silicon atoms to produce an alloy which would not overheat. His solution has never been bettered, and silicon steel has remained to this day the standard material for the construction of all electrical motors.

Once at Purdue, Fessenden found himself with the time and the facilities to pursue his own interests. His infectious passion for research and for the potential of new technologies, along with his education in the classics and his considerable skill as a linguist, made him a very popular lecturer. Fessenden's new position was short-lived, though, as less than a year after he began, George Westinghouse endowed a new chair of electrical engineering at the University of Pittsburgh and recommended that his former employee be offered the position. In September 1893, Fessenden took up his new post and entered what has been described as the most productive and creative period of his life, a time during which he became obsessed with the notion of radio telephony — voices transmitted without wires.

Yet while the famous Guglielmo Marconi began to fire his wireless messages over the Salisbury Plain and across the English Channel, Fessenden struggled merely to transmit across his laboratory. He tinkered endlessly with his equipment, always improving it, but was never quite satisfied. The instrument that caused him the most grief played a crucial role in receiving signals and could not be dispensed with. Called a coherer, the small tube contained tiny iron filings that reacted to each individual incoming signal by lining up in a fashion similar to filings exposed to a magnet, forming a bridge which allowed the small spark to pass. Just barely adequate for transmitting Morse code, it seemed almost useless for Fessenden's purposes. It could not react nearly fast enough to capture the subtle complexity of voice messages.

Even as he worked at replacing the coherer with something better, however, Fessenden realized that he had to grapple with a much more fundamental problem. He still did not have an adequate grasp of the theory behind wireless transmission. Although he knew that signals could be beamed from a transmitter and that they would cause some reaction in a receiver, neither he nor anybody else in the world clearly understood what happened in between.

Fessenden's conclusion about the true nature of radio transmission came during a train ride. After exhausting months of research, he finally fit the pieces together as he rode from Toronto to Peterborough, Ontario, where he was enjoying a much-needed vacation. Wireless signals, he decided, did not need to be mere blasts of energy rocketing straight from the transmitter to be caught by a receiver. Treated properly, they would form a continuous wave emanating from the source and spreading out through the air like ripples from a pebble dropped into the water. Morse code could already be sent by starting and stopping the waves — long blasts for dashes and shorter ones for dots. But far more important, Fessenden determined that voice or even music could be carved onto a continuous stream of waves and carried across the open air to a receiver.

TWIN RADIO TOWERS, COBB ISLAND EXPERIMENTAL SITE

His continuous-wave theory provided the insight that set Fessenden apart from others who struggled with the secrets of wireless transmission. For one thing, he now knew exactly why the coherer could not work. And he also knew precisely what he had to do: design a machine capable of producing an endless signal of radio waves, carriers for his voice messages.

As Fessenden envisioned, radio waves work like an invisible conveyor belt. The message placed at one end travels along until it is scooped up by a receiver. The belt continues to move even when nothing is being carried. If no message is transmitted, then only silent radio waves travel through the air. Fessenden demonstrated that the sound waves of voices or music could be made to change the shape of the radio waves like a message scratched onto the surface of the conveyor belt and thus could be carried over great distances. At the source, he "added" sound waves to the radio waves, and at the receiving end, he "subtracted" the radio waves, leaving the sound message intact.

Fessenden returned to Pittsburgh in late August 1896 charged with

THE BASE OF THE TOWER, BRANT ROCK, MASSACHUSETTS

renewed passion and confidence. He plunged back into his research, quickly bending old ideas and technical theories to fit his new understanding. The experiments brought a string of successes, and by November, Fessenden and his assistant Mr. Kintner had begun to cover fresh ground. In a few months, he progressed further than he had in all the years before, redesigning much of the machinery he needed in the process. Yet even the research time available to him as a professor was not enough for his purposes. As word of his experiments spread, he began looking for a better position.

By March 1900, Reginald, Helen and their 8-year-old son Reginald Kennelly, along with their cat and a new research assistant, were installed at Cobb Island, in the Potomac River . In a demonstration for the U.S. Weather Bureau, Fessenden had so impressed his audience with the ease with which his wireless system could transmit and receive Morse code that he was hired at an annual salary of $3,000. Settled into crude accommodations on the island, he set up his equipment and soon had his invisible messages winging out over the land and the sea.

FESSENDEN, SEATED, AND THE BRANT ROCK STAFF, JANUARY 30, 1906

Fessenden startled even his employers with the clarity of the Morse code messages he transmitted back to the receiving tower that had been erected at Capitol Hill in Washington. The first year-long contract proved such a success that the operation expanded, and the Weather Bureau sent Fessenden on to Roanoke Island, off the coast of North Carolina. As the number of stations increased, he continued his own research into wireless telephony.

Eventually, Fessenden secured private financial backing from a pair of Pittsburgh millionaires named Thomas H. Given and Hay Walker Jr. Together, they formed the National Electric Signaling Company and set up a research station at Brant Rock, on the coast near Boston, Massachusetts. But the story of Fessenden's work on the coast — on Cobb and Roanoke islands and finally at Brant Rock — is not only a tale of scientific research and glorious success but also a pitiful list of broken contracts, manipulation and dishonesty. Only Fessenden's great physical strength and endurance saw him through the former; only his strength of character sustained him through the latter.

Both the Weather Bureau and his later partners ignored Fessenden's vision of transmitting voice without wires: each considered telegraphy the only important goal. Radio was an impossible dream, they said, at best a useless toy. Nonetheless, Fessenden carried on his work in secret. He had no trouble keeping his backers satisfied, because with each improvement to his voice equipment, his telegraph system also benefited. Sending dots and dashes, in fact, was becoming child's play for the machinery he had dubbed the "Fessenden System."

Just nine months after arriving at Cobb Island, Fessenden orchestrated the world's first voice transmission. Two moves and two years later, on January 3, 1906, he made the first successful two-way transatlantic telegraph transmission only days after the erection of his towers. He was also the first to send voice across the ocean and the first to make a long-distance transmission over land, from Brant Rock to New Orleans, in 1906. And on Christmas Eve of the same year, he made the first broadcast from a single transmitter to several receivers at once. Like the broadcasts of the radio stations that would one day blanket the continent, his Christmas Eve programme included both music and conversation. His unlikely audience consisted of sailors on United Fruit Company cargo ships, which carried equipment for receiving Morse code messages listing the changing big-city prices for their products. The sailors steaming north from the tropics must have suspected a divine Christmas miracle when their telegraph machines suddenly broke into speech and then sang them a song. The voice they heard, however, was that of Reginald Fessenden himself, beaming out from his radio towers at Brant Rock, first reading from the Bible and then playing the violin as he sang *O Holy Night*. Edison's phonograph — itself still a rather novel item — was also used to play Handel's *Largo*.

It was during frenzied preparations for the historic broadcast that another of Fessenden's minor inventions came in handy. Throughout his career, Fessenden's active imagination threw off ideas like spinning fireworks. To control the clutter on his desk, he had invented microphotography, and to summon his staff from the various buildings at the Brant Rock site, he invented a version of the pocket pager, which users placed in their headgear. One day, hats started buzzing all over the station. Workers rushed to the 400-foot main transmitting tower, where they discovered their distinguished employer stuck fast in a cylinder surrounding the ladder to the top of the mast. Comfortable living had given Fessenden a girth to match his impressive stature. Un-

OPERATORS AT THEIR POSITIONS, BRANT ROCK

fortunately, he had become just an inch too large around the middle and was now wedged tightly into the ladder passage. On the brink of making history, the world's greatest radio pioneer had to be stripped naked and rubbed with grease so that he could slip back down to the ground. Instead of shedding weight, however, Fessenden chose to rig up a bosun's chair on the outside of the tower, and he completed his preparations swinging in midair, 400 feet above the ground.

The first transatlantic voice transmission, a far greater accomplishment than a mere broadcast, had, in fact, occurred accidentally a month before the eventful Christmas. Fessenden himself learned of it when he received a registered letter from his assistant Mr. Armor at the Machrihanish station in Scotland: "At about 4 o'clock in the morning, I was listening in for the telegraph signals from Brant Rock when, to my astonishment, I heard, instead of dots and dashes, the voice of Mr. Stein telling the operators at Plymouth how to run the dynamo. At first, I thought I must be losing my senses, but I am sure it was Stein's voice, for it came in as clearly as if he were in the next room." Weeks and months of intensive labour had gone into establishing contact across the ocean, and it had happened unintentionally. But before a formal demonstration could be arranged, an early December storm brought the Machrihanish tower crashing to the ground. The epoch-making Christmas broadcast was conceived simply to fill in the void left by the disaster in Scotland.

Technical setbacks and accidents, however, could not compare with the human greed and shortsightedness that also pursued Fessenden and his family and assistants. He parted company with the Weather Bureau when his immediate superior tried to force him to sign over some of his precious patents. Since Fessenden had sunk every available penny into his experiments, the patents he registered were the only item of value he possessed to secure his family's future. And yet, upon leaving the government station at Roanoke Island, Fessenden assigned his patents to the company he formed with Given and Walker. Although their backing allowed Fessenden to perfect his system, the businessmen effectively cheated Fessenden out of his due by manipulating contracts and by insisting that instead of developing the equipment and selling it to customers, they should try to sell the whole system to a large communications company or to one of the armed services.

Given and Walker's ill-advised marketing strategy allowed Fessenden's spectacular achievement to drain slowly and sadly away. Other companies rushed to exploit his inventions, and soon, hundreds of his patents were being violated. His ideas made fortunes for people who had had nothing to do with their development.

Although these business dealings brought Fessenden only frustration, it was also a time of great excitement and accomplishment. Under Fessenden's direction, huge towers were erected. He designed and built machinery unlike any the world had ever seen, including an alternator supplied to him by the General Electric Company, which he rebuilt, increasing the speed from 12,000 rpm to an unheard-of 70,000 rpm. And on Roanoke Island, fate arranged what was surely one of its strangest coincidences. As Fessenden worked on one side of the small sandy island to perfect the radio technology that would change the world in a matter of years, two men he befriended on the island were hard at work on the opposite shore. They, too, had plans for the future that were often met with skepticism. But Fessenden listened in fascination as Wilbur and Orville Wright described their experiments with aviation at Kitty Hawk.

The years following Fessenden's final great successes at Brant Rock in 1911 slowly filled with frustration. The business machinations of Given and Walker threatened to rob Fessenden of his patents, and the long years of court battles began. The Canadian government stifled his attempts to establish a wireless company in his own country and instead provided support to Marconi. Although Marconi's system by this time looked like a crude toy compared with Fessenden's perfected system, the Marconi company had the support of the British government and was therefore backed by the Canadian government as well.

By 1912, the family fortunes were at a low ebb, and even Fessenden had to admit that the future looked grim. Nonetheless, a chance meeting with Mr. Fay of the Submarine Signal Company of Boston turned the situation around. Asked if his experience with radio could have a bearing on underwater communication, Fessenden almost immediately made himself indispensable to the small company. Within months, he had revolutionized his new field; in less than two years, he had transformed theoretical speculation into hardware.

Because waves cannot travel through water in the same fashion as they spread through the air, Fessenden had to completely reinvent his equipment. Waves sent pulsing through the water bounce back from any solid object they encounter; based on that fact, only a few short months after the *Titanic* rammed an iceberg and plunged to the ocean floor, Fessenden came up with a solution to the problem that had plagued the shipping industry for centuries. A high-frequency underwater sonic oscillator lay at the heart of the system. Equipment that recorded the time it took for a series of waves to bounce back to the ship proved able to give an accurate measure of the distance to a mountain of ice floating in the darkness. By pointing the equipment straight down, Fessenden demonstrated that even the depth of the water could be accurately ascertained. Fessenden foresaw a day when a captain could simply glance at a gauge to determine how much room there was between his keel and the dangerous rocks or sand and mud at the bottom of the ocean.

With the outbreak of World War I in Europe, Fessenden immediately volunteered his services to the Canadian government. He sent a list of his qualifications and inventions — a remarkable document — offering not only his skills but free access to the technology he had created. Fessenden then turned his talents to the grim subject of modern warfare. He developed what he called the visible bullet — "tracer

CREATING A RADIO SIGNAL, BRANT ROCK

bullets," as they are now known. He designed a lighter and more powerful internal-combustion engine, an enemy-artillery detector, an improved gun sight and even a system for locating enemy zeppelins using his wireless technology. He spent months in England meeting with the people who could promote his inventions. The King himself sent representatives to request that Fessenden develop his direction-finding antenna into a working system for the defence of London.

During World War I, supply ships crossing the North Atlantic had no protection against submarines; warships could not fight off the enemy because they were unable to locate their underwater attackers. As hundreds of thousands of tons of shipping sank and hundreds of young men were drowned in the cold northern waters of the Atlantic, Reginald Fessenden knew that he had the answer.

The same equipment that could pinpoint icebergs and accurately sound the ocean depths, he determined, could also locate submarines. Yet Fessenden was repeatedly blocked in his attempts to demonstrate his equipment to the U.S. Navy. Fessenden and the Submarine Signal Company even went so far as to install equipment — at their own expense — on a navy destroyer in order to conduct tests. The gear worked perfectly, successfully locating a submarine that had been lost during the preliminary trials. And yet the Submarine Board, the body of experts established to oversee wartime developments in submarine technology, ordered half of the equipment removed from the vessel before the official test commenced. Inexplicably, the board continued to block Fessenden's efforts for the remainder of the war. Helen Fessenden recorded the events in bitter detail, but neither she nor her husband ever discovered why his life-saving technology was kept from those who needed it. Like so many of his other inventions, it became standard equipment in the years following the Armistice.

In 1921, Fessenden offered the U.S. Navy another small device distilled from his encyclopaedic knowledge of electricity and radio waves. This machine, in addition to transmitting and receiving voice messages, also sent a visual image. The navy, predictably by now, rejected this offer too, and in 1926, an Englishman named John Baird won enduring fame as the inventor of television. In fact, Reginald Fessenden, the minister's son from East Bolton, Quebec, had held U.S. patents on just such a machine since 1919.

Following the war, Fessenden returned to his experiments with depth gauges and designed the Fathometer, the miraculous piece of equipment he had foreseen in 1912. Before long, it had become standard shipboard equipment. For the first time in the long history of maritime travel, captains could determine the depth of the water below them quickly and accurately.

In the subsequent years, Fessenden watched as his wildest prophecies about the wonders of radio were met and surpassed. The technology he had conceived and developed sparked a worldwide revolution. By 1922, there were 600 commercial broadcasting stations and over a million listeners in the United States alone. Communication, mass media and the constantly accelerating flow of information began to shape the 20th-century world into something entirely new. And in large measure, these changes sprang from the heart and mind and dreams of one remarkable man.

On March 31, 1928, the Radio Trust of America gave up its court battle with Reginald Fessenden. Companies around the world now used his inventions. A whole industry rested on the foundations he had created, and the violations of his patents were too numerous to count. Although he had sought $60 million in reparations, he settled, in the end, for $2.5 million. While the amount represented only a fraction of the true value of his creations, the settlement brought an end to the interminable legal battles that had overshadowed so much of his professional life.

The money dispelled Fessenden's lifelong fears of impoverished retirement. He and Helen retired to a comfortable home in Bermuda, where Fessenden spent his final years studying and writing down his own long-held theories about Ptolemy and the ancient Greeks. In Bermuda, the Fessenden family home once again became a laboratory where he conducted experiments on everything from horticulture to an electric therapy designed to strengthen his own failing heart. He died there on July 22, 1932.

Well over six feet tall, broad-shouldered and ever greater of girth as he grew older, Reginald Fessenden had matched his towering physique with a powerful mind. Yet two great mysteries surround his life: how was he able to produce so many brilliant inventions, and how did he fail to gain the recognition he deserved? According to George Vosper of Queen's University at Kingston, Ontario, the early experiments in Edison's laboratories provide an answer to the first question. After years spent studying Fessenden's life and accomplishments, Vosper concluded that Fessenden's model of the atom, his understanding of the electrical forces at work in all matter, provided him with unique insight. While the greatest physicists of the age were still struggling with atomic theory, Fessenden leapfrogged ahead and reduced their tentative theories to practical working hypotheses. He knew something about the nature of the world that other people did not, and it allowed him to travel quickly over unexplored terrain.

Just as the work of great scientists occasionally leads them to useful inventions, Fessenden, the untrained inventor, made at least two outstanding contributions to the world of pure science. He unlocked the essential secrets of the atom, and years later, while the rest of the world—including Bell, Edison and the great pioneer Marconi—still believed that wireless worked by transmitting blasts of energy like the cracking of a whip, Fessenden correctly concluded that electromagnetic *waves* carried radio messages through the ether.

The greed of businessmen who pirated his patents may very well account for Fessenden's relative obscurity. For the first 15 years of commercial radio development, many of the companies involved faced lawsuits launched by Fessenden's attorneys, and the companies did their best to downplay the inventor's central role in the development of the technology that was making them wealthy. And for his part, Fessenden did not do much to ingratiate himself. He wasted little of his formidable energies on patience, and to most, he appeared an arrogant, intolerant man who gained a reputation as someone very hard to work with. Unlike Edison and Marconi, who had both established prosperous businesses bearing their names, Fessenden never became publicly associated with a large-scale, successful public venture. No company ever stood to profit by keeping his name before the public eye.

Fessenden was undoubtedly the victim of both financial and historical injustices, but Helen Fessenden, while defending her husband, unwittingly points out that he himself never took the time to win over people who might have handed him the credit he deserved. Her partner was never a difficult man to *work* with, she explained, but "he was an intensely difficult man to play politics with. Nothing seemed to him so futile." So although Reginald Fessenden lived a life of dynamic activity, crowned with unprecedented achievement, he died without winning the spectacular fame he deserved.

WILLIAM STEPHENSON

THE WIREPHOTO

On D-day, June 6, 1944, as the armies of the United States, Canada and Great Britain swarmed over the beaches of Normandy, an unusual man was riding as the tail gunner of a bomber flying overhead. At 48, William Stephenson had been waging war against the Germans for more than a quarter of a century. A scientist, a millionaire, an inventor and an influential Canadian industrialist, Stephenson was nonetheless an anonymous figure as he soared over the battles on the beaches below. Not until 30 years later would it become widely known that he was also one of the principal coordinators of British intelligence in World War II and a powerful figure in the Allied war against Nazi Germany.

Like Stephenson himself, his flight over a war zone was something of a puzzle: a chief intelligence officer typically works behind a desk, not in the whirling confusion of a full-scale invasion. Although analytical and scholarly in his manner, however, Stephenson possessed great physical stamina and courage in the face of immediate danger.

William Stephenson enlisted in the Royal Canadian Engineers in order to fight for the British in World War I, 15 years after his father had joined the Manitoba Transvaal Contingent and left the family home at Point Douglas, near Winnipeg, Manitoba. William Stephenson Sr. died in South Africa during the Boer War, leaving behind a wife, a successful lumber-milling operation and a 3-year-old son who, without a father, was forced to grow up quickly.

The key to William Stephenson Jr.'s future success can be found in his youth. In school, he excelled in mathematics. At home, he shared responsibility for the family business. He developed a keen interest in new technologies, experimenting with kites and steam engines, and was fascinated with airplanes and flight. He also built his own telegraph, which he used to communicate with ships travelling on the Great Lakes more than 500 miles away. A voracious reader, he was already a well-educated and competent young man when the century's first great clash of European nations broke out.

Stephenson's initiation into military conflict was as a foot soldier in the hellish trenches of World War I. Barely 19 years of age and already commissioned as a second lieutenant, he survived 20 months in the mud and filth of the front lines. Men were wounded, blinded and blown apart under heavy bombardment. Poison gas floated over the carnage. Unimaginable casualties sucked away any romantic sense of adventure, and soldiers went mad under the brutal pressures.

Within a year, Stephenson had been promoted to captain; before many more months had passed, he, too, was caught in a gas attack. With his lungs damaged, he was sent back to England and listed as "disabled for life." A strong sense of loyalty prevented him from accepting the retirement that had been forced upon him; told that he would never again be fit for fighting, Stephenson managed to obtain a transfer to the Royal Flying Corps (RFC). After only five hours of flight training, he was assigned to 73 Squadron.

STEPHENSON, 73 SQUADRON

At first a competent but undistinguished pilot, Stephenson was galvanized into action after being badly shot up by a pair of enemy fighters. In a period of weeks, he took down several German planes and a pair of kite balloons, becoming well known not only to his colleagues in the air force but also to foot soldiers who recognized his plane as he dropped low over the fields, dipping his wings in greeting.

Stephenson flew his last mission on July 28, 1918. The same incident that ended his career as a fighter pilot and won him the Distinguished Flying Cross and the Military Cross also indirectly launched his postwar career as an industrialist and financier.

On that date, Stephenson was flying a lone patrol when he spotted a French reconnaissance plane under attack. With the benefit of surprise, he shot down two of the enemy craft and crippled a third before the rest dispersed. But when he flew in beside the observation plane for identification, the French gunner, in momentary confusion, fired on Stephenson, wounding him and hitting his engine. Stephenson nursed his plane to the ground but landed behind German lines, where he was wounded again in the leg as he tried to cross into British territory. Taken prisoner, he was eventually sent to a prisoner-of-war camp at Holzminden on the River Weser, near Brunswick.

The loss of any skilled pilot was a serious blow to the British effort, and the Germans took special precautions to keep RFC prisoners locked away. Stephenson made several unsuccessful attempts to escape before he settled on an effective strategy. By exaggerating the pain in his wounded leg, he convinced his jailers that he could not possibly slip away from them, thereby winning himself a measure of freedom within the camp. In October 1918, a few weeks before the Armistice, he succeeded in cutting through the wire and making his way back to his squadron in France. Although his career as a fighter pilot had come to an end, the period of captivity had provided one unexpected benefit. During his stay in Holzminden, Stephenson happened upon an ingenious can-opening device that, due to wartime complications, had been patented only in Germany, Austria and Turkey. Upon his return to Canada at the war's end, he improved the can opener's design and patented it worldwide. That effort provided him with a small fortune and served as the financial basis for his postwar activities.

Before the end of the war, though, Stephenson had attracted the attention of his superiors within the British military and political hierarchy. His level-headed analyses of combat conditions, submitted in regular reports, had eventually landed on the desk of Admiral Sir Reginald Hall, who had taken an interest in the young wing commander. Hall believed that the Armistice of 1919 might very well represent only a pause in the European conflict, and he recognized that changes in technology would inevitably shift the focus of both political and military strategy. Working to maintain Britain's intelligence networks and to ensure that they kept pace with the times, he earmarked William Stephenson for a role in British intelligence.

Stephenson enrolled at Oxford University before his return to Canada, as well as at an institution that was a precursor to Cranwell Aeronautical College. There, he resumed his early interest in communications, and radio replaced telegraphy as the object of his fascination. Back in Manitoba, he failed to find support for popular broadcasting and spent his time studying government attempts at public radio while supporting himself by teaching mathematics and sciences at the University of Manitoba. But Stephenson was not merely a dabbler in the world of science and technology. His later entrepreneurial achievements and his much debated and controversial involvement in espionage tend to obscure the fact that he began his career as a successful scientist.

In the 1920s, radio was still a mystifying electrical device to most people. The first commercial radio station in the world, KDKA in Philadel-

STEPHENSON STATIONED IN FRANCE

phia, began transmitting in 1921, and over the next decade, the public gradually became accustomed and devoted to the voices and music that travelled for miles and found their way out of the rough speakers in their homes. Radio began to change the world, shrinking distances and knitting communities together with an easy distribution of information and entertainment. And as mass communication took its first faltering steps, scientists chased after new applications for the technology. A wireless enthusiast since his youth and now trained in communications technology, William Stephenson joined the ranks of inventors and radio pioneers.

Since the early 1850s, scientists working with wireless technology had suspected that if coded sounds could be communicated, it should also be possible to send visual images over distance. Thirty years before Stephenson took up the problem, engineers had devised a crude system of dividing photographs into tiny squares and then coding each section according to its relative darkness or lightness. After this information had been transmitted, the image could be "reassembled" at the receiving end. Even after years of experimentation and improvement, however, the result remained unsatisfactory. Simple line drawings could be successfully transmitted, but the complex tones of a black-and-white photograph could not. The process interfered with the subtle variations of shadows and greys and black, giving the finished picture a rough, patchy appearance. Journalists desperately wanted a process that could transmit photographs quickly, but the results of the early technology remained unusable.

With his usual combination of imaginative insight and practicality, Stephenson grasped the theoretical solution to the problem and set about designing the necessary machinery. When he failed to secure the financial backing he needed for practical experimentation at the University of Manitoba, he continued to work on the theoretical details. He reasoned that since human interference — dividing a photograph into sections and assigning values to each — had caused insurmountable problems, a method had to be found which would allow the picture itself to dictate the information transmitted. A machine that was capable of "reading" the photograph — scanning the image and reacting to the variety of shades which make up the complete picture — was required.

The technology of photo transmission begins with the fact that different shades reflect different amounts of light. A clean, white surface returns most of the light shone upon it, while a black surface reflects very little. If the same amount of light is shone on the two surfaces, the strength of the two reflections will be measurably different. Stephenson realized that if he could determine the amount of light returning from a given point on a photograph, he would have an exact indication of the shade of grey at that specific point. The reflection itself contained the necessary information. If he could measure the light from every point on the photograph, then he would have a series of signals describing the whole picture. The required apparatus for photo transmission would therefore combine two features: it would be capable of scanning the picture, sending out a controlled beam of light to pass over every point on the photograph, and it would also be able to record instantaneously the different amounts of light bouncing back from the surface, converting that information into an electric current.

In the early 1920s, Stephenson returned to Britain to pursue this venture. He bought an interest in two manufacturing companies, Cox-Cavendish and General Radio Company, then quickly turned to the problems of photograph transmission. He began work in the General Radio laboratories at Twyford, where his experiments soon attracted the attention of London's *Daily Mail*. The newspaper's management fully understood the potential benefits of wireless photography and had been doing its own research since 1908. They decided to support Stephenson in his efforts and provided him with the services of Professor T. Thorne Baker, an eminent research chemist and photography expert.

Stephenson's first step was to modify an existing scanning device patented by the German physicist Paul Gottlieb Nipkow in 1884. Instead of using Nipkow's single rotating disc, Stephenson combined two of the round plates, each with a series of precisely spaced slits cut into it. The two overlapping discs were arranged and synchronized so that as they turned, different pairs of slits lined up with each other, one after another, and a strong beam shining through them appeared as only a tiny, moving spot of light which travelled back and forth across a photograph placed in front of the machine. Each time the light moved over the width of the photograph, it dropped slightly lower on the page, until the whole image had been scanned. The spot moved smoothly over all the shadings of black and grey and white, and the intensity of the reflection from this light varied continuously as first one tiny area and then the next was illuminated. That solved the first half of the problem.

At the time Stephenson was conducting his experiments in Twyford, scientists already knew that an element called selenium responded to light by giving off an electrical charge. A great deal of study had been devoted to this "photoelectric" phenomenon. Because small amounts of light stimulated a weak charge and more light created a greater charge, selenium seemed to be a perfect solution. The material should be able to measure the strength of reflections from the photograph, and in principle, it provided Stephenson with exactly what he needed. Selenium, however, had one important drawback. The grey, crystalline substance reacted very slowly, and it could not keep pace with a spot of light that was continually shifting. Hence, in practical terms, it was useless for simultaneous image transmission. Stephenson had to find his own substitute.

The second stage of the project cost Stephenson many hours of careful research and painstaking experimentation. Later developments in television and related fields would make photoelectric-cell technology commonplace, but in the early 1920s, that information did not exist. Stephenson's achievement is therefore all the more remarkable. In the end, he managed to produce an instrument that not only converted light into electrical currents but did so virtually instantaneously, registering each change in the amount of light that entered it and making a corresponding adjustment to the signal it gave out. He called this a

THE ADVANCED WIRELESS PHOTOGRAPH TRANSMITTER, 1922

"light-sensitive device," and by combining it with his system of rotating discs, he completed the photo-transmission apparatus. A photograph scanned by the machine was translated into signals that could be sent out over radio or telephone lines. A receiver reversed the process by unscrambling the transmission, then precisely controlling the amounts of light necessary to produce an exact copy of the photograph.

Because of its support, the *Daily Mail* earned the right to publish the world's first wirephoto. On December 27, 1922, it announced that as a result of a "great scientific event . . . a new era in illustrated journalism is beginning."

Stephenson's photo transmitter became an immediate commercial success. A photograph taken anywhere in the world could be sent off to the newspapers of major cities, where it would arrive almost instantly, communicated by means that were both accurate and inexpensive. Newspapers clamoured for the new apparatus, and Stephenson's patents made him a wealthy man. His invention changed the face of journalism, and although improvements were later incorporated, the basic technology remained unaltered for another 50 years.

As Stephenson himself knew, his machine also laid the groundwork for the inventors of television. As early as 1919, he was writing papers on the subject of transmitting and receiving moving pictures, and while his wirephoto technique required 20 seconds to reproduce a single still photograph, he explained that the next important step would be just a matter of time. His invention moved the world closer to communication technologies that would transform forever the way people live.

The 1920s marked an astonishing period of intense creativity and excitement for Stephenson. He became one of a loose fraternity in Great Britain whose common goals were the advancement of radio science and the technological preparation for a possible renewal of war in Europe. He met with radio manufacturers and shared his observations of Manitoba's government-run broadcasting station. He realized that a similar British endeavour would not only provide a valuable service but also create a need for home receivers, and he encouraged the formation of the British Broadcasting Corporation (BBC). His interest in Cox-Cavendish and General Radio enabled him to corner a share of the burgeoning home-radio market.

Home radio was a phenomenon that greatly appealed to thousands of eager customers. People could switch on the new devices in their homes, and voices spoke. Music could apparently be drawn out of thin air, and what had previously been a scientific toy quickly became an essential new technology that promised rapid and exciting developments. The early success of the BBC meant much more than increased radio sales. It also guaranteed continuing research in the field of communications. Stephenson was ideally suited as a leader of the new industry. His own inventive flair and his ability to appreciate the accomplishments of others, combined with the drive necessary to produce commercial success, ensured funds for more research.

Although William Stephenson eventually shifted his energies from the laboratory to the boardroom, his success did not dull his appetite for science and new technologies. His newfound wealth gave him freedom, and his conviction that Britain must prepare for continued war in Europe gave him a sense of purpose. Charles Proteus Steinmetz, a man whom Stephenson considered "a mathematical genius," was offered the free use of laboratory space. Chaim Wiezmann, another scientist and, like Steinmetz, a German political refugee, also came to work for Stephenson. Exploiting the intellectual challenge these men provided, Stephenson wove exciting new ideas into his commercial successes.

With his colleagues, Stephenson probed the edges of science, searching for the technologies of the future. It was an incredibly productive period of history, and Stephenson moved within a community of scientists and engineers who, while still grappling with some of the basic theories of radio, were designing the tools of future wartime and peacetime: faster and safer planes, radar, lasers, jet engines and television.

In the years between the two world wars, Stephenson's wealth grew as he diversified. He acquired interests in the fast-growing automobile-manufacturing industry, in developing films and in sound recording, and he founded Earl's Court Ltd. in order to build the famous hall and stadium. Through the Electrical and General Industrial Trust, he channelled funds into researching and constructing planes, despite the fact that Britain's governments were steadfastly avoiding any military development. He owned steel factories in Scandinavia, coal mines in the Balkans and oil refineries in Romania, and in England, he controlled Catalina Ltd., one of the first plastics companies. His vast industrial and commercial empire included everything from Pressed Steel, a company that provided 90 percent of the car bodies used by British auto manufacturers, to Alpha Cement Co. and Sound City Films, whose Shepperton Studios produced over half of the British films made in the 1930s. His interests were international, and his wealth and influence became a considerable responsibility, one which he took seriously.

Stephenson's financial success rested on his ability to recognize the economic potential of new technologies. Inventive ideas fired his imagination; and not content simply to exploit the work of others, he dedicated his growing resources to assisting in research and development.

Despite his personal prosperity, Stephenson remained concerned about the need for military preparation. A decade passed, and the 1930s brought the rise of Nazism in Germany, where Stephenson's significant business interests gave him access to the records of companies being used to illegally re-arm the German nation. While his companies and laboratories continued to work on projects that would provide the groundwork for a new technology of warfare, Stephenson himself became increasingly active. At Berlin University in 1933, he watched as the works of Thomas Mann, Sigmund Freud and Albert Einstein were consumed in the great bonfires of the infamous Nazi book burnings.

His fears deepened, and he took another step into the secret war that preceded the open hostilities.

Stephenson became an important member of Focus, an unofficial collection of people concerned with British complacency and its lack of defence preparations. Although secretly supported by King George VI, the group's aims were at odds with public opinion, and its members had to work covertly to avoid accusations at home of trying to force Britain into another devastating European war. Along with Winston Churchill, Admiral Hall and others, William Stephenson became the centre of much of this activity.

Even in the early days of his career, Stephenson had little taste for publicity. His conspicuous and varied successes, along with a dramatic record of action from World War I, made him a natural object of curiosity, yet he remained quietly out of sight. As his unofficial tasks became ever riskier and more vital, he withdrew further. The influence of powerful people helped to discourage the inquisitiveness of the press, and in 1935, Stephenson dropped from public view completely. Even old clipping files disappeared from newspaper libraries. In his new role, Stephenson reached out through his vast business operations and seized upon any bit of information that might help in the war to come. He travelled unobtrusively through prewar Europe in the guise of a level-headed businessman interested in discussing the future of industry and willing to listen carefully to the new leaders of the emerging Third Reich as they proudly listed their economic successes. He heard German military leaders boast of the new blitzkrieg technology, the machinery of "lightning war," which, they confided, would someday be used to crush the "Bolshevik menace" in the east.

Stephenson's espionage activities during World War II have since become the stuff of unreliable legend. Although it appears that the level of intimacy and trust he enjoyed with world leaders has been exaggerated, it is true that he became a crucial engineer of American support for Britain at a time when the United States remained officially neutral and when the American voting majority did not intend to become involved in the European war. From an office in New York City, Stephenson ran the British Security Co-ordination (BSC), a secret intelligence organization that operated throughout the world for the duration of the war. At the peak of its activities, over 30,000 people served William Stephenson. Members of the nobility, professors, clerks and famous actors gathered the bits of information that eventually fun-

WILLIAM SAMUEL STEPHENSON

nelled into his hands. Stephenson worked 20 hours a day, seven days a week, supervising everything from diplomatic exchanges at the highest level and romantic intrigues designed to cull information from staff members of the Italian and Vichy French embassies in Washington to the logistics of monitoring virtually all of the mail travelling from the United States to the European continent. The BSC guarded against German espionage activities in North and South America, encouraged and supported resistance movements in German-occupied countries and ran a training camp in Canada on the banks of Lake Ontario for commandos and assassins. Stephenson received no pay for his work and, over the course of the war, spent more than $1 million of his own money on BSC operations.

In personality and training, Stephenson was ideally suited to his unusual task. The war that began in 1939 unfolded into a conflict unlike any before it. It became an economic war of unprecedented scope, a murderous extension of precisely the kind of competition that Stephenson had already mastered in becoming a very wealthy man. His incredible energy and his calm, analytical approach kept him on top of the massive workload, and his own war experience had taught him a healthy respect for the consequences of his hidden activities.

World War II marked the beginning of technological warfare. New machines made traditional battle tactics obsolete. France's Maginot Line, prepared as the ultimate defence against the trench warfare that had raged 20 years earlier, fell without a struggle. The Germans swept past and around the elaborate system of fortifications in tanks and trucks. Rather than marching massive armies across the countryside shoulder to shoulder, the German leaders had smaller units spearhead attacks and pounce on strategic positions while the main body moved into position behind them. Where once a battlefield lay within the generals' view, it now stretched for hundreds of miles.

Fast, engine-driven carriers increased the speed of armies, but it was another invention of the 20th century that changed warfare completely. The Nazi blitzkriegs, the vast beachhead landings at Normandy, coordinated long-range bombings and the far-flung battles of North Africa all relied entirely on quick, accurate communication. Radio had changed forever the ways that people kill one another. The dreams of radio pioneers like Guglielmo Marconi and Reginald Fessenden and Stephenson himself, men who had learned to draw voices out of the empty air, now had hardened into the new reality of war.

Keeping track of the German race to devise new technologies became the responsibility of the BSC, and Stephenson's lifelong interest in the theories of emerging technologies made him an invaluable broker of information about German progress. At the war's end, Stephenson was knighted by King George VI, and when Britain closed down the BSC's New York office, he returned once more to a prosperous private life until his death in 1989.

The story of William Stephenson's life weaves together the threads of science, commerce, war and espionage, creating a pattern that closely resembles the history of the 20th century itself. He played a crucial role in some of the greatest military and peacetime developments of his time. For over 50 years, he lived behind a veil of secrecy, half-truths and deception, and as a result, few will ever know the full, unembroidered story of his life. Without doubt, however, it is the story of a man whose many skills and inventive talents helped to change the world.

J. ARMAND BOMBARDIER

TRIUMPH OVER WINTER

J. ARMAND BOMBARDIER AT AGE 9

Joseph-Armand Bombardier loaded the first Ski-Doo ever made into the trunk of his car and set out on the first leg of his journey to northern Quebec. The mild spring weather of 1952 threatened to strip away the last of the deep winter snows around Valcourt, Quebec, home of the multimillion-dollar snow-machine company L'Auto-Neige Bombardier. Its founder and president, who had designed and built the new machine, wanted more time to test it: the perfect winter vehicle, the happiest achievement of Bombardier's long career.

He travelled north by car and train and then airplane to James Bay. Five hundred miles from Montreal, he found the snow he needed. He fired up the awkward-looking little machine and zipped away across the deep snow faster than a person can run on dry ground, faster than a team of dogs can pull an empty sled, faster than anyone had ever moved over level snow. Before he had completed his first circuit, a crowd had gathered to watch the excitement, and when Bombardier returned, first one and then another and another of the local hunters and trappers took a turn on the magically self-propelled sled.

Over the next few days, Bombardier served as mechanic while these snow-travel experts put his machine through its paces. The lightweight sled with the powerful little motor and patented wide rubber track didn't need roads or clearings. Trappers and hunters drove the tiny Ski-Doo into snow that only dogsleds could travel, through deep drifts and along the twisted trails of the forests. Bombardier kept a careful record of the comments they made. No better test could have been designed for a machine that had to be a dependable aid to Canadians working and living in harsh winter conditions.

Armand Bombardier's career looks to many like nothing more than the quiet, steady expansion of a successful private business. At first glance, there is little evidence of the remarkable personality behind the name that was to become synonymous with snow vehicles and winter

TOY TRACTOR BUILT BY THE 13-YEAR-OLD FUTURE INVENTOR

recreation. But hindsight smooths the edges of even the most interesting stories; in the case of Armand Bombardier, it hides the fact that in his lifetime, he completely changed the winter lives of people who live in any of the world's cold climates by transforming impassable and sometimes deadly snowdrifts into a smooth blanket, an endless roadway over which snowmobilers can travel anywhere at all.

Born on April 16, 1907, on a farm in rural Quebec, Joseph-Armand Bombardier was the eldest son in a family of eight. Always content to keep his own company as a youth, he passed many of his happiest hours in the farm woodworking shop, where he built himself a lathe and spent his spare time piecing together small mechanized toys for himself and his brothers from leftover materials. He learned his school lessons well, but it was his time in the shop that taught him both patience and rudimentary mechanics. And as he worked at his projects, he learned to love solving the puzzles buried in a motor that would not run or unlocking the mystery of how machines work.

While Bombardier was still a teenager, his father sold the farm and moved the family into the nearby town of Valcourt, where he bought the general store. Armand settled easily into town life. He earned money running deliveries for his father. Without the responsibility of farm chores, he had extra time and energy to build and design and experiment. But moving into town also meant that the eldest son would not inherit the farm and thereby carry on a family tradition. Other plans were called for, and in September 1921, at the age of 14, Armand was enrolled in St. Charles Borromée Seminary in Sherbrooke, Quebec. There, his mechanical talents were no help at all. The whirling of gears, the mysteries of steam engines, clockworks and internal combustion, all of the things that his mind grasped with intuitive ease, were buried under an avalanche of classical studies — Latin, mathematics and ancient Greek. For almost three years, he persevered, keeping up with his schoolwork and burying his frustration. But the young inventor knew he would never be happy as a priest, and the holidays became times of long-anticipated and merciful release.

Away from school, Armand was like a young workhorse freed from the traces and set loose in the field. He resumed his experiments, often with more enthusiasm than wisdom. In the summer of 1922, he built a small steam engine, which he powered with air pressure from an inflated automobile tire. Hooked up to his aunt's spinning wheel, it almost tore the wheel from its mounts. Armand even took his engine to a team of steamfitters working in town and had them run steam into the tiny machine, which of course whirled like a thrashing demon before it blew up entirely. That same summer, he and his brother Leopold did their best to blow themselves up with a homemade welding torch — a tin can with a nozzle and an old tire pump for pressure into which Armand poured gasoline, making it a better bomb than a cutting tool. By the fall, he already had plans for his first snow machine.

That first snowmobile is now the stuff of legend. Stories are told of how Armand and his younger brother successfully piloted the thundering machine down the streets of Valcourt, scattering pedestrians and horses before crashing headlong into the side of a barn. The brothers did not, in fact, collide with anything, but they were wisely ordered by their father to dismantle the machine. Armand's first effort at a vehicle that could travel over snow was a vicious contraption composed of an automobile engine mounted on an old sleigh with a huge, hand-carved wooden propeller affixed to the radiator fan shaft. The steering mechanism consisted of ropes tied to the front runners of the sleigh, and the propeller stuck out behind like a whirling meat grinder, with no protection for passengers or pedestrians. The wonder was not so much that the motor sled worked but that no one was chewed to bits.

It soon became obvious to everyone which direction Armand Bombardier's future should take. (Perhaps his parents decided it was better for their son to train properly as a mechanic than to continue at the

THE FIRST SNOW MACHINE: AN ENGINE AND PROPELLER ON SKIS

seminary; if his holiday hobby went on much longer, somebody was going to get hurt.) In any case, in the springtime of Armand's sixteenth year, he became a mechanic's apprentice. He leapt into the miraculous world of engines and mechanical wizardry, first in the town of South Stukely and then in Montreal. He watched eagerly, and he listened and learned. During the day, his hands acquired the smooth, practised dexterity of a skilled mechanic, and at night, he pursued his own education programme, studying electrical engineering and mechanics by correspondence and reading journals that told him of the latest technological developments and scientific discoveries. Bombardier saw technology as the magical key to a better future.

By the 1920s, it was clear that automobiles would occupy an important place in that bright future. Cars were no longer merely toys for the wealthy, and Bombardier realized that back in his hometown — even though Valcourt boasted only 3,000 inhabitants — they would soon need a mechanic to run a garage just like those in which he worked in Montreal. Since cars and farm machinery needed constant repair, there would always be plenty of business. In May 1926, after three years of training, Bombardier moved his tools and textbooks into a small garage that his father had built for him. At the age of 19, he took the first steps down a road that, unbeknown to him, would lead to unimaginable success, wealth and fame.

It makes perfect sense that Armand Bombardier, the mechanic-inventor, would make his first snow machines out of cars. And in the 1920s, it also made sense that horse-drawn sleighs would play a role in his earliest efforts. Before snowploughs and salt and before better roads and improved automobiles, virtually all winter travel involved the use of sleighs. The regular traffic wore deep runner grooves in the snow, which in well-travelled areas acted like inverted railroad tracks, guiding the traffic along the roads. As he looked out from the door of his already thriving small repair business and auto garage, Bombardier reasoned that a car which fit into the same grooves would also be steered along and be able to travel in the snow. Accordingly, Bombardier modified the front axle and steering mechanism of a car he had acquired for the purpose and, after further thought, added a second rear axle and stretched chains around both rear wheels. With the good traction he achieved and the groove-guided steering at the front, Bombardier discovered to his great satisfaction that he could take his winter car anywhere that sleighs travelled the roads.

Thus he began a yearly pattern that continued for the next decade. In the spring, summer and fall, he tended to his flourishing repair business and established a mechanic's most important asset — a good reputation. A growing assortment of tools lined the walls of his shop, and in his office, textbooks and journals filled the shelves. He hired his brother, his uncle and a brother-in-law; he even took on a partner who sold cars. But each winter, as business slowed, Bombardier returned to his growing obsession, bringing a patience and determination to his experiments with snow machines that would last through the years.

To a visitor, the village of Valcourt, Quebec, on a sunny winter day must have seemed a magical place. Deep snow blanketed the houses and streets, and wood smoke drifted from the chimneys. Bells rang as horses pulled people and goods about in sleighs. And then the village inventor — no doubt looking to some like a mad scientist — would come into sight in a thundering contraption, a car clipped off at the wheels and raised up onto skis and a clanking steel track. In his next attempts, Bombardier narrowed the rear wheels and replaced the front wheels with skis that again fit into the sleigh tracks. He also substituted the chains on the rear wheels with a heavy steel track that made the car look

THE 1929 SNOW CAR, A MODIFIED MODEL T FORD

more like a modern bulldozer than anything else. In 1927, Bombardier sold one of these cars to Charles Boisvert, a local hotelier who used it to carry customers to and from the train station. Between 1928 and 1930, he produced a dozen more.

But Bombardier's life was not completely restricted to the world of invention. In his early twenties, he began to think of marrying and starting a family. Despite a reputation for reckless driving and somewhat eccentric behaviour, he nevertheless successfully wooed and married Yvonne Labreque, a young woman who had lived in Valcourt all her life. By the time the couple had had two sons, Yvonne understood that her husband's work often came first. The two facets of Bombardier's life came tragically together, however, when his 2-year-old son Yvon suffered an acute attack of appendicitis on a snowy winter night. Summoned to Yvon's bedside from the garage, where he spent the evenings designing and building "snow cars," as he called them, Bombardier realized that there was no way to get his dying son through the snow-blocked roads to the hospital in Sherbrooke. Back at his garage, the awkward-looking machines he had been working on were strewn about in useless, unassembled pieces. His son's death was a cruel irony that lent profound determination to Bombardier's ambitions.

By the 1930s, Bombardier had learned a great deal about what made a good snow vehicle. Simply modifying cars was not enough. He became increasingly inventive and, over the next few winters, produced a series of new experimental machines. In 1933, after years of training and experience, having studied aeronautical engineering and made observations during his own experiments, he returned to a design quite similar to the reckless propeller sled that he and his brother had piloted down the streets of Valcourt when Armand was only 15. He had learned a thing or two since then about aerodynamics — and comfort — and this time, the propeller drove a tiny, streamlined two-seater that sat up on skis front and back. He began the crucial move away from converting automobiles and instead designed his vehicles from the ground up. In fact, automobile manufacturers of the time might have picked up some points about body design if they had taken the time to study the efforts of this Quebec inventor. Snow travel required stricter attention to weight and weight distribution, and Bombardier's 1934 model had all of the swept-back styling and design of later racing cars. Even standing still, it looked like a needle poised to cut cleanly through the air.

Snow cars were one thing, but Bombardier envisioned a vehicle that could leave the road and travel freely anywhere there was clear space and snow. Step by step, he compiled the features he needed. Skis were essential, and so was an elongated traction track, rubber now instead of steel, in place of wheels, which only make contact with the ground at one small point on their rounded surface. By placing the engine in the rear, he achieved even greater traction, and although each of his experimental machines, from the converted snow cars onward, had worked, it was only in 1935 that he finally had something that he was confident would perform well in a variety of snow conditions.

Four years earlier, the Benedictine monks of Saint-Benoit-du-Lac Monastery had appeared at Bombardier's workshop and asked to be taken for a drive in his snow machine. They were so impressed that they purchased one on the spot and thereafter could be seen making their winter rounds in Armand Bombardier's rattling contrivance. It proved to be the finest kind of advertising. Even though several of the Benedictine brothers had almost fallen through the ice after attempting a shortcut over a frozen lake, word continued to spread of *les auto-neiges*. By the time Bombardier had perfected most of the design features, inquiries were coming from across the country about the machines that could tame the roads and wild snows of winter. Already the workshop contained all the tools and machines he needed, and now potential customers were seeking him out. Nonetheless, it represented a bold step when Bombardier decided to close down his successful garage and devote all his energies to producing the kinds of machines that had filled his imagination for so long. He and his staff began work in earnest, and Bombardier confronted the new task of actually selling enough machines to support himself and his family.

JOSEPH-ARMAND BOMBARDIER

The man who had designed and built the vehicles, with the help of a staff he had also trained, now decided to become his own chief salesman. He packed his bag, loaded it into the spacious cab of his 1935 model and set out to drive around the province. No salesman could have been more sincere about his product. In his promotion efforts, Bombardier hit upon the perfect combination of showmanship and frugality. Instead of buying advertising, he simply drove into a town and invited the local newspaper editor or reporter for a ride. He then whisked his passenger away on a dash down the winter roads and over fields. The next day, the product he wanted to sell would be spectacular front-page news: a vehicle with a heated cabin that replaced snowshoes or horses floundering in snowdrifts and could seemingly travel anywhere. Wherever he went, Armand Bombardier and his snow vehicle left a trail of excitement.

From the beginning, his company proved a great success. The only things more plentiful than Bombardier's ideas were his customers, and as he designed more ski-cars, ski-trucks and ski-buses for multi-passenger use, people snapped them up. Modern roads and snow-clearing techniques eventually made many of the Bombardier vehicles less necessary, but in the 1930s, they unlocked the winter world, carrying goods to customers and children to schools in almost any kind of weather.

B-7: THE BOMBARDIER SEVEN-PERSON SNOW VEHICLE

Bombardier named the most popular of his early production models the B7 — B for Bombardier and 7 for the number of passengers it held. He called it his "original heavy workhorse," and with several hundred pounds of Ford V8 engine sitting directly over a pair of Bombardier's now-patented rugged steel and rubber tracks, there were very few winter conditions that could stop it. His tiny enterprise, renamed L'Auto-Neige Bombardier, began to blossom and diversify. He acquired a team of salesmen across the province — competent mechanics like himself who could provide reliable service as well as distribution. Even in the final years of the Great Depression, Valcourt, Quebec, began to bustle. The Bombardier company recruited ever larger numbers of local workers and trained them in the skills of manufacture and mechanics. Although each machine was handmade, the Bombardier team was producing nearly 100 units per year. Then came World War II.

The war temporarily brought a dramatic halt to Bombardier's plans, but it also proved beyond a doubt that his ingenuity and industry had earned him wide respect. Like other large and specialized manufacturers, his services were commandeered by the war effort. Tanks already formed an important part of the modern Canadian arsenal, but

BOMBARDIER WORLD WAR II ARMOURED TROOP TRANSPORT

Bombardier's track system and construction techniques could be modi-fied to create an all-terrain vehicle. In the snowy northern battlefields of Europe, the brainchild of the inventor from tiny Valcourt would give Allied troops an important newfound speed and manoeuvrability. The Canadian government asked him to design a winter troop carrier, and Bombardier promptly modified his B12 model, adding artillery mounts and oversized tracks as well as extra doors and a hatch on the roof. It won immediate approval. In conjunction with army engineers, he proceeded to develop several new machines. And although commer-cial sales of his own products were restricted by the wartime govern-ment, the Bombardier operation continued to expand: 150 troop car-riers with added armour were built in Montreal and sent overseas. They were followed by one of Bombardier's most revolutionary vehicles, the legendary Penguin, a sleek, low-profile body slung over wide tracks that extended the full length of the machine and flared up at the front, ready to surmount any obstacle. Designed to confront far more than just snow, it was unstoppable, adaptable to virtually any conditions and terrain. Compared with the comfortable, rounded form of his buses and snow cars, the Penguin did indeed look like a stark military ma-chine, and from the snows of northern Europe, the influence of Bom-

PROUD INVENTOR OF THE MUSKEG TRACTOR

bardier's machines now reached as far south as the Mediterranean and even into the South Pacific.

The war could have spelled disaster for someone in Bombardier's position. His inventions were protected by patents, but the war years swallowed up much of the precious time available before emerging competitors would legally be able to copy his ideas. Contracts with the government, however, had also strengthened the company and enabled it to expand its operations, and now Bombardier the ingenious inventor also had to become a canny businessman and marketing strategist. Sales boomed in the years immediately following the war, but as roads and automobiles improved, the demand for his large snow machines inevitably declined. The answer, Bombardier recognized, was careful diversification—new machines designed to solve other kinds of problems.

Bombardier's snow machine, shaped like a giant jellybean with thundering tracks and tiny skis sticking out in front, was now adapted and sometimes completely redesigned for use in a bewildering variety of exotic locales. Bombardier filled contracts for the French Foreign Legion and gave them vehicles for use in the Sahara Desert. After studying the problems of the logging industry, he designed machines capable of powering themselves into the bush and being loaded with large piles of logs. Orders came from Peruvian sugarcane plantations, where mud, not snow, made travel impossible by ordinary means. Bombardier machines were used to lay oil pipe in Scotland. And Bombardier designed one of his most famous vehicles for use by oil-exploration crews in western Canada. The Muskeg Tractor, named for the deep northern bogs of ancient leaves and moss, could be driven over swampy areas where even a person walking might sink waist-deep into the muck. Sir Vivian Fuchs, the Antarctic explorer, returned the Muskeg Snowmobile to its native element in 1957 and travelled over Antarctic snows to the South Pole with a speed and comfort that had never before been imagined. He described his Bombardier machine as "outstandingly rugged, even at 60 below," and added, "We all have great affection for the Muskeg."

All of his adult life, Armand Bombardier had laboured earnestly to design practical, useful vehicles: machines that conquered the winter snows, delivering mail or schoolchildren or emergency service; machines to carry lumberjacks deep into the bush and to push oil exploration into the northern wastes. Yet because of his last great invention, the Ski-Doo, Bombardier's name, for most people, conjures up images of winter fun.

The inventor's name might well have disappeared along with his large round-backed Quebec snow cars, remembered only in frontier regions as a line of heavy equipment. However, the postwar years brought two developments that would prove essential to Bombardier's continued success and to his permanent place in the history of invention and technology.

The first was economic prosperity. Suddenly, thousands of Canadians had money to spend on recreation. The timing was critical. Bombardier introduced his "Ski-Dog," or "Ski-Doo," as it was quickly renamed, onto the market at just the time when people could afford to buy such a machine, more often for the simple pleasure of whisking over the snow than for work of any kind. A booming economy helped to make Bombardier's name a household word.

The second crucial factor in the eventual success of the Ski-Doo was the rapid progress in small-engine technology brought about by World War II. Under the pressures of war, materials and virtually every aspect of engine design improved dramatically. Combined with Bombardier's track system and experience with snow travel and ski steering, the new small motors helped to produce the ultimately versatile snow machine. The single (and sometimes double) track of the new design meant that it could be steered by the driver simply leaning to either the left or the right. Its lightness and precise weight distribution meant that the machine could, in many cases, float over, rather than plough through, the snow. So sophisticated was Bombardier's vision that the snowmobile's basic concept, shape and design has never varied significantly from Ski-Dog #1, which Bombardier took north to James Bay for testing.

Any concern about L'Auto-Neige Bombardier's ability to survive the setbacks caused by the war was dispelled once the public discovered the little sled Bombardier had modestly hoped would be useful to missionaries, trappers, woodsmen and farmers. Sales increased by more than 100 percent for each of the first several years of production. Even as competitors jumped in with their own models, Bombardier had to find a way each year to produce more than twice as many machines as he had the year before. By 1965, there were over 50,000 snowmobiles in use, and Bombardier's company alone was turning out 15,000 more per year. The hardworking, sober-minded inventor from Valcourt, Quebec, had unintentionally precipitated the most exciting new winter sport the world had seen in centuries, and across the North American snowbelt, snowmobile clubs sprang up, sponsoring everything from leisurely day trips to oval-track competitions, rallies, sprints and marathon cross-country races.

For all his worldly success, Armand Bombardier preferred the quiet, full life he had created for himself in Quebec's Eastern Townships — spending time with his family, hunting with his friends, participating in community events and devoting the lion's share of his time to design and innovation. Blessed with a cool, practical business sense, Bombardier made every decision only after carefully weighing each option, all the while maintaining the strictest quality control in his own operation. While his machines took the Bombardier name around the globe, he rarely strayed from his hometown, and as his company prospered, so did Valcourt. Profits from the business flowed through the community. The village that had watched and encouraged its own eccentric native inventor grew into a small, prosperous modern city as Bombardier's snow machines found enthusiastic markets around the world.

Indeed, the groundwork Bombardier laid for his company was so

THE FIRST SKI-DOO, APRIL 1959

sound that L'Auto-Neige Bombardier was stable enough to survive and continue to thrive despite the death of its founder in 1964. Eventually, whole teams of research-and-development personnel were formed to carry on the work that Joseph-Armand had begun alone in his tiny Valcourt garage. The family business, made into a public company in 1969, has since expanded into almost all fields of transportation technology. The young man who wistfully studied aeronautical journals in his spare time spawned an empire that eventually provided parts for NASA's lunar modules.

But the real story of Joseph-Armand Bombardier is of the man who took his first snowmobile into northern Quebec to test it under realistic conditions and to hear the advice of those who would benefit most by its creation. Bombardier knew from years of experience how ideas and drawings translated into meshing gears and smooth-running machinery. His inventive imagination could turn flickering possibilities into new realities. But he possessed other traits as well. He did not simply dream wild dreams of wondrous inventions. He was a native of rural Quebec who saw snow travel as a problem and a challenge to be overcome. Neither fame nor fortune was as important as surmounting the obstacles he encountered, and surmount them he did, with persistence and enthusiasm. Rather than merely dispatching an eager employee or two to conduct the test trials of his latest invention, he went himself. A businessman who had built a hugely successful company, Armand Bombardier nonetheless saw his life in more practical terms: he bent his skills to the task of producing vehicles that would improve the lives of those who confronted rugged Canadian winters.

Success and wealth were not nearly as interesting to Bombardier as was machinery, how it worked and how it could be made to work better. By the time he had boarded his plane in northern Quebec to return home in the spring of 1952, Bombardier had a list of modifications for his new winter vehicle. Left behind with a local trapper was the prototype of the first modern snowmobile. The machine that sparked a revolution in winter travel and recreation eventually found its way into a museum; but first, it saw 10 years of the hard trapline use for which it was designed. That was the measure of Joseph-Armand Bombardier's success.

FURTHER READING

ABRAHAM GESNER

Barkhouse, Joyce, *Abraham Gesner*, Fitzhenry & Whiteside, Don Mills, 1980.

Gesner, Abraham, *New Brunswick, With Notes for Emigrants*, Simmonds and Ward, London, 1847.

SANDFORD FLEMING

Burpee, Lawrence J., *Sandford Fleming, Empire Builder*, Oxford University Press, London, 1915.

Grant, George M., *Ocean to Ocean*, James Campbell and Son, Toronto, 1873.

Howse, Derek, *Greenwich Time and the Discovery of Longitude*, Oxford University Press, Oxford, 1980.

Maclean, Hugh, *Man of Steel: The Story of Sir Sandford Fleming*, The Ryerson Press, Toronto, 1969.

Thomson, Malcolm M., *The Beginning of the Long Dash*, University of Toronto Press, Toronto, 1978.

GEORGES-ÉDOUARD DESBARATS AND WILLIAM LEGGO

Desbarats, Peter, *The Canadian Illustrated News* (Commemorative Portfolio), McClelland & Stewart, Toronto, 1970.

Eder, J.M., *History of Photography*, Columbia University Press, New York, 1945.

Gernsheim, Helmut and Alison, *The History of Photography, From the Camera Obscura to the Modern Era*, McGraw-Hill, New York, 1969.

Greenhill, Ralph and Birrell, Andrew, *Canadian Photography, 1839-1920*, The Coach House Press, Toronto, 1979.

Singer, Charles, ed., *A History of Technology*, Clarendon Press, Oxford, 1958.

Taft, Robert, *Photography and the American Scene, A Social History*, Dover Publications, New York, 1938.

MABEL BELL AND THE AERIAL EXPERIMENT ASSOCIATION

Bruce, Robert V., *Bell: Alexander Graham Bell and the Conquest of Solitude*, Little, Brown & Company, Boston, 1973.

Eber, Dorothy, *Genius At Work: Images of Alexander Graham Bell*, McClelland & Stewart, Toronto, 1982.

Green, Gordon H., *The Silver Dart*, Brunswick Press, Ltd., Fredericton, 1959.

Parkin, J.H., *Bell and Baldwin*, University of Toronto Press, Toronto, 1964.

Toward, Lilias M., *Mabel Bell, Alexander's Silent Partner*, Methuen Publications, Agincourt, 1984.

THOMAS WILLSON

Precious, Carole, *Carbide Willson*, Fitzhenry & Whiteside, Don Mills, 1980.

Union Carbide Canada Ltd., *Carbide, Saga of a Canadian Inventor*, Toronto, 1976.

REGINALD FESSENDEN

Fessenden, Helen, *Fessenden: Builder of Tomorrows*, Coward-McCann, Inc., New York, 1940.

International Telecommunication Union, *From Semaphore to Satellite*, Geneva, 1965.

Raby, Ormond, *Radio's First Voice*, Macmillan of Canada, Toronto, 1970.

WILLIAM STEPHENSON

Hyde, H. Montgomery, *The Quiet Canadian*, H. Hamilton, London, 1962.

Stevenson, William, *A Man Called Intrepid*, Harcourt, Brace, Jovanovich, New York, 1976.

JOSEPH-ARMAND BOMBARDIER

Brown, J.J., *The Inventors: Great Ideas in Canadian Enterprise*, McClelland & Stewart, Toronto, 1974.

Precious, Carole, *Bombardier*, Fitzhenry & Whiteside, Markham, 1984.

GENERAL

Brown, J.J., *Ideas in Exile, A History of Canadian Invention*, McClelland & Stewart, Toronto, 1967.

Nostbakken, J. and Humphrey, J. *The Canadian Inventions Book*, Greey de Pencier Publications, Toronto, 1976.

Williams, Trevor I., *The History of Invention, From Stone Axes to Silicon Chips*, Facts on File Publications, Oxford, England, 1987.

INDEX

PHOTO CREDITS

Alexander Graham Bell National Historic Park: p. 67, p. 68, p. 71, p. 72, p. 77, p. 79, p. 80. *Margo Stahl*: p. 42. *Musée J. Armand Bombardier*: p. 136, p. 137, p. 139, p. 141, p. 143, p. 144, p. 145, p. 146, p. 149. *National Archives of Canada*: p. 17 (Imperial Oil Collection PA103280), p. 31 (C8692), p. 33 (C1670), p. 34 (PA22130), p. 37 (C2787), p. 39 (C14128), p. 44 (C2789), p. 49 (PA51846), p. 50 (C48503), p. 55 (C79300), p. 58 (PA22256), p. 61 (C48501), p. 87 (C53493), p. 90 (C53503), p. 93 (C53494), p. 94 (C53495), p. 95 (C53491), p. 97 (C53489), p. 98 (C53499), p. 132 (PA141575). *New Brunswick Museum*: p. 20, p. 23, p. 27. *North Carolina Division of Archives and History*: p. 105, p. 109, p. 110, p. 111, p. 113, p. 116. *Reprinted from THE QUIET CANADIAN, H.M. Hyde, Hamish Hamilton, London, 1962*: p. 123, p. 125, p. 128.